Gateways to Glory!

(Gates in Christian Experience)

Robert L. Sumner

Gateways to Glory
Copyright © 2007
Biblical Evangelism
5717 Pine Drive
Raleigh, NC 27606

Cover Design by
Ron Sumner

ISBN 10: 0-914012-38-X
ISBN 13: 978-0-914012-38-2

Printed in the United States of America

Dedication

To the Lovely Lady God Brought Into My Life
After Both Our Mates had Gone to Heaven

"Dottie" Sumner, Bible Teacher Par Excellence

the former Mrs. Neil Holm, Mother of 8, Grandmother of 30,
Great-Grandmother of 8 (and counting)

Table of Contents

Foreword

There are many phases of the Christian life. Certainly the first and most important step is securing our eternal destiny. Jesus Christ died, was buried, and rose again on the third day in order to provide us with an opportunity to spend eternity with Him in Heaven. And by accepting His payment for our sins, we can be rescued from Hell. Since Jesus has done all the work, our job is easy ... we simply have to make a choice.

For many of us however, the real challenge begins *after* we've become born again. How will we live the rest of our days while we're here on this earth? Can we discover God's will for our life? Is it possible to lead a victorious life? *Gateways to Glory* offers a unique perspective into how to best maximize our growth as Christians. By using the names of the ten city gates of Jerusalem as illustrations as outlined in the 3rd chapter of Nehemiah, Evangelist/Author Robert L. Sumner demonstrates how God has preserved in His Word a very relevant series of lessons for today's developing Christian.

I heartily recommend this book to everyone who wants to be an effective Christian in a confused world that is lost and rapidly disintegrating.

Dr. Tim LaHaye
Noted Author, Educator,
BibleConference Speaker

Introduction

This series of studies is based on the ten gates in the city of Jerusalem as listed in Nehemiah 3. While that historic biblical city had more than ten gates – and some were known by different names – I believe the Holy Spirit of God, who supervised the writing of that biblical book, directed Nehemiah to list only the ten he did and to use the names he did in order to preserve a special lesson for our Christian era. The opening chapter, "Nehemiah's Example," is an introductory lesson based on Nehemiah 1.

I claim no originality for the idea behind the gates, which applies them to a natural progressive order in today's Christian experience. The beloved Harry Allen Ironside, pastor for nearly two decades at the historic Moody Church in Chicago, was the first one to see these divine lessons – as far as I have been able to ascertain, at least – setting forth the idea in a single message, "The Gates of Jerusalem." Since that time, I have noted any number of preachers doing the same; that is, preaching a single sermon on the ten gates in Nehemiah 3, making the application of Christian experience.

I was so impressed with the idea, back in the early 1940s in the midst of World War II and during my first pastorate at Pontiac, Illinois (now the Calvary Baptist Church), that I decided to preach a series of sermons on the subject. Starting on October 10, 1943, and concluding – with interruptions for a missions conference, Thanksgiving, Christmas, and New Year's messages – on January 16, 1944.

As the preacher, my heart was so thrilled with these studies that I repeated the series, with modifications of course, in a couple of later pastorates. And now I am bold enough, with fear and trembling, to release them in this more permanent written form.

If these studies of the Jerusalem gates prove as much of a blessing to you as it has been to me, I will feel amply rewarded for the trouble I have expended to make them available in a book format.

Chapter 1

NEHEMIAH'S EXAMPLE

"The words of Nehemiah the son of Hachaliah. And it came to pass in the month Chisleu, in the twentieth year, as I was in Shushan the palace,

"That Hanani, one of my brethren, came, he and certain men of Judah; and I asked them concerning the Jews that had escaped, which were left of the captivity, and concerning Jerusalem.

"And they said unto me, The remnant that are left of the captivity there in the province are in great affliction and reproach: the wall of Jerusalem also is broken down, and the gates thereof are burned with fire.

"And it came to pass, when I heard these words, that I sat down and wept, and mourned certain days, and fasted, and prayed before the God of heaven,

"And said, I beseech thee, O LORD God of heaven, the great and terrible God, that keepeth covenant and mercy for them that love him and observe his commandments:

"Let thine ear now be attentive, and thine eyes open, that thou mayest hear the prayer of thy servant, which I pray before thee now, day and night, for the children of Israel thy servants, and confess the sins of the children of Israel, which we have sinned against thee: both I and my father's house have sinned.

"We have dealt very corruptly against thee, and have not kept the commandments, nor the statutes, nor the judgments, which thou commandedst thy servant Moses.

"Remember, I beseech thee, the word that thou commandedst thy servant Moses, saying, If ye transgress, I will scatter you abroad among the nations:

"But if ye turn unto me, and keep my commandments, and do them; though there were of you cast out unto the uttermost part of the heaven, yet will I gather them from thence, and will bring them unto the place that I have chosen to set my name there.

"Now these are thy servants and thy people, whom thou hast redeemed by thy great power, and by thy strong hand.

"O Lord, I beseech thee, let now thine ear be attentive to the prayer of thy servant, and to the prayer of thy servants, who desire to fear thy name: and prosper, I pray thee, thy servant this day, and grant him mercy in the sight of this man. For I was the king's cupbearer."

– Nehemiah 1:1-11

American streets are unsafe to walk on at any speed. Rapes, muggings, hold-ups, killings, kidnappings, gang war shootings and other crimes are commonplace on the national scene. Every new crime statistical release from our FBI in Washington makes the last one seem like "the good old days."   The problem has long since passed the alarming stage and has become frightening; yea, *terrifying!*

Trying to keep pace with lawlessness, America's social ills are skyrocketing: alcoholism, drug abuse, divorce, homosexuality, abortion, euthanasia, child molestation, unmarried couples living together, and child pornography/molestation are setting all-time high statistics – *and no one seems to care!*

We had better face the truth: *our homes and our churches are not getting the job done!* Kids raised on the Dewey-Spock permissiveness philosophies have never learned the meaning of restriction. They have been told they are entitled to do as they please, and they believe it. Laws they do not like or do not agree with may be broken, their leaders have assured them. Things are going to get a lot worse before they get better – *if they get better at all!* It is not necessary to be a prophet or the son of a prophet to understand this fact. It is the simple law of sowing and reaping set forth in the Word of God.

What Jehovah said of Judah and Jerusalem in the days of Uzziah, Jotham, Ahaz and Hezekiah is timely for our nation today: "Ah sinful nation, a people laden with iniquity, a seed of evildoers, children that are corrupters; they have forsaken the Lord, they have provoked the Holy One of Israel unto anger, they are gone away backward" (Isaiah 1:4).

America needs – desperately – *what the old-timers called "a Heaven-sent, gully-washing, stump-floating, Heaven-sent, Holy Spirit revival!"*

It might be well to subtitle the opening chapter of this work, "The Christian and His Church's Need," because we are going to make applications from the situation in Nehemiah's day for the circumstances and needs of our own day. If you are satisfied with the *status quo*, unconcerned about your church's need, then this message is not for you. Quite the contrary, this chapter is for saints who want to see great things done for God, Satan soundly defeated, souls won to Christ and then baptized, Christians edified and built up in the faith – and all the rest that goes with a church triumphant.

Get the scene of our text firmly fixed in your mind. It was approximately 90 years after Cyrus' decree which permitted the Jews, led by Zerubbabel, to return to Jerusalem, occupy the city, and rebuild the temple. About a decade before the time of our text, Ezra had led another expedition, permitted by the decree of Artaxerxes, and had been instrumental in bringing revival to the people, restoring the law and the sacrifices.

Nehemiah hadn't gone back to the Promised Land with the others, remaining instead in Persia. We cannot say why he hadn't gone, but he had risen to a position of honor, trust and favor with King Artaxerxes. Called the king's cupbearer, his rank within the palace was somewhat like a presidential press secretary today. But even though he had not returned to Israel, he was nevertheless a devout Jew, one who loved and served the Lord God, Jehovah.

The colorful British evangelist, Gipsy Smith, used to say that those who worship God could be divided into four classes. First are the *ankle-deep* Christians. They come to church once a week; usually, on Sunday morning. You can't count on them for anything else, although they have no problem going to the theater, sporting events and all the rest as often as they please. There are no restrictions on these latter matters; that is something else entirely for these part-timers.

Second are the Christians who get in *up-to-their-knees*. You can count on them to be present for Sunday school and church in the morning and back again on Sunday night. They even come occasionally on Wednesday night for prayer meeting. But that is it. Don't count on them for anything else; their spirituality is limited to keeping pews warm.

Third in the crowd you will find those who are *up-to-their-loins*. The strength of their moral fiber is Christ. They live according to Christian principles, pursue paths of purity, practice separation standards, and give to the causes of the church. God bless them.

Finally, however, you will find a small minority who get in *up-to-their necks*. These are the dear ones who live to serve Christ. The church is not a sideline with them; they are present whenever the doors are open. Their private and public lives are beyond reproach and pastors everywhere rise up and call them blessed. They keep the church machinery running and do whatever they are asked, often seeing things needing to be done and doing them without being asked. They are all in, totally absorbed with the things of God and His church.

Nehemiah was in that fourth group, a man sold out to Jehovah God and seeking His glory in everything. That is why he reacted as he did when word came to him about the sad conditions in the holy city, learning that the remnant there was "in great affliction and reproach: the wall of Jerusalem also [was] broken down, and the gates thereof are burned with fire" (Vs. 3). He had just received a firsthand account of the sorry situation from Hanani, one of his relatives, and some of the other brethren of Judah. Having just arrived in Shushan directly from Jerusalem, the story was burning in their hearts and on their minds. How graphically they presented it to Nehemiah!

A firsthand account does something to you that nothing else can. For example, you may have picked up your newspaper some time ago and read the tragic story of that drunk who was driving on the wrong side of an interstate highway in Kentucky and hit head-on a church bus loaded with young people returning from a church outing, turning their vehicle into a fiery funeral pyre, burning beyond recognition nearly 30 of those precious souls. You were surely horrified and shocked at the time, but, in all probability, you dismissed it from your mind and haven't thought of it again until faced with this reminder.

However, if one of the survivors of that terrible accident told you the account, that surely would be an entirely different story. When he described the sudden screech of rubber on concrete, the horrifying impact of steel upon steel, the shattering of glass, the sudden explosion of the gas tanks, the blazing sheets of flame racing from one end of the bus to the other, the scrambling of the few for the emergency exit door in the rear, the blinding denseness of the black smoke, the screams and cries of the trapped victims, the heat of the flames, the awful stench of burning human flesh, the sudden ushering of those dear ones into eternity without any advance warning whatsoever – you would not forget it in a few minutes. Surely the memory would live on to haunt you for months, years, decades – probably you would never be able to completely erase it from your mind.

Nehemiah received the latter kind of eyewitness report and found it heartrending. That once great, proud, mighty city so awesomely feared by all her enemies far and near was now laughed at, jeered, ridiculed and despised by those same enemies. In addition, Jerusalem stood in grave danger of invasion at any time, since her walls were broken down, her gates had been burned with fire, and she had no defense, no protection. It was, indeed, a pathetic situation.

When Nehemiah got to Jerusalem and saw it for himself, this is how he described it: "Ye see the distress that we are in, how Jerusalem lieth waste, and the gates thereof are burned with fire: come, and let us build up the wall of Jerusalem, that we be no more a reproach" (2:17). Note his words: distress, waste, burned, reproach.

Remember, Nehemiah was a Jew. It was his duty to do something about the pressing problem. By the same token, we are Christians and it is up to us to do something about the pathetic conditions prevailing at present in our churches all over America. And since we are in the same predicament today as Nehemiah was in 446 BC, let us examine carefully what he did and profit thereby.

First, we see,

I. GENUINE CONCERN!

Verse 4 quotes Nehemiah as saying, "It came to pass, when I heard these words, that I sat down and wept, and mourned certain days, and fasted, and prayed before the God of heaven." His concern manifested itself four ways.

A. He "Wept!"

The concern had gone past his head and had journeyed down deep into his heart. His tears were more than the kind Americans shed when a tragic – and usually fictitious – tale is being told on television or in the theater. The latter kind of grief is merely sympathy, not concern.

Nehemiah *wept!*

Before our churches are built up or we see genuine revival, the concern we share must lodge deep in our hearts. In all honesty, how often do you weep over the condition of your church?

Be honest now, *do you **ever** weep?*

We need the spirit of a Jeremiah, who said about the situation in his day, "Oh that my head were waters, and mine eyes a fountain of tears, that I might weep day and night for the slain of the daughter of my people!" (Jeremiah 9:1). And he said again, "For these things I weep; mine eye, mine eye runneth down with water, because the comforter that should relive my soul is far from me: my children are desolate, because the enemy prevailed" (Lamentations 1:16).

Why emphasize weeping? Because a concern that does not break the heart and cause the fountains of the soul to be broken up through tears is really not much of a concern. Nehemiah shed honest, sincere tears.

There is an old story about General William Booth, the founder of the Salvation Army, who received a pathetic communication from one of his captains regarding the situation on a certain field, and how he had tried everything he knew to bring about change, but without success. He begged the godly general to tell him what to do.

Booth wired a terse two-word response: **"Try tears!"**

That will work when all else fails.

B. He "Mourned Certain Days"

Evidently this period of mourning lasted about four months. It began in the month Chisleu, during the twentieth year of Artaxerxes' reign (1:1), and it was the month Nisan of the same year (2:1) when Nehemiah went into the king's presence – and then a chain of events took place that resulted in his leading another expedition to Jerusalem. Chisleu was the third month and Nisan the seventh on the Jewish calendar.

Day and night, continuously, constantly, without intermission, his thoughts were of the needs of the holy city, Jerusalem. And every time he thought, he wept and mourned.

Does the need of your church, the concern for revival in your community, have an effect on you like that? It should. If it did, after awhile we would find ourselves doing something about it, just as Nehemiah did!

C. He "Fasted!"

We do not hear much about fasting any more and mighty few modern saints ever get involved with it. Our churches have days of feasting ("dinner on the grounds, with all the trimmings"), but mighty few of fasting. Yet Jesus said of the faith that moves mountains, "This kind goeth not out but by ... fasting" (Matthew 17:21). No wonder so few mountains are moved by today's churches.

Some of our politicians call for fasting more frequently than do our pulpits. In the midst of the dark, despairing, difficult days of the Civil War, President Abraham Lincoln appealed to the nation "to recognize the sublime truth announced in the Holy Scriptures and proven by all history, that those nations only are blessed whose God is the Lord." So he called for April 30, 1863 as a day of national humiliation, fasting, and prayer.

His proclamation said, in part:

> *"Intoxicated with unbroken success, we have become too self-sufficient to feel the necessity of redeeming and preserving grace, too proud to pray to the God that made us!*
> *"It behooves us, then, to humble ourselves before the offended Power, to confess our national sins, and to pray for clemency and forgiveness."*

Are Christians in the 21st century too self-sufficient, too proud to humble ourselves before the Almighty in fasting and prayer?

We often speak of how Jonathan Edwards preached his famous sermon, "Sinners in the Hands of an Angry God" – and 500 were converted to Christ on the spot! But seldom is it mentioned that for three days prior to that event Edwards had not eaten one morsel of food as he fasted, and for three nights he had not closed his eyes in sleep as he wrestled with God in prayer.

If Christ called for fasting (Mark 2:20; Matthew 17:21), and the Apostle Paul was "in fastings often" (II Corinthians 11:27; see also 6:5), who are we to ignore it? Some of the most noble names in Christendom – such as Martin Luther, John Knox, John Calvin, John Wesley and Charles Finney – were men who believed in, often preached about, and personally practiced fasting.

In Bible times, fasting was a natural response to life's problems. When Esther had to go into the king's presence at the risk of her life, what did she tell Mordecai and the Jews in Shushan to do? She begged them *to fast* for three days and three nights (Esther 4:16)!

When Jehovah, through His servant Joel, called for repentance on the part of the people of Judah, what did He say? "... turn ye even to me with all your heart, and *with fasting*, and with weeping, and with mourning" (Joel 2:12, emphasis added).

When Daniel, in his study of prophecy, wanted to know more about the 70 years Jeremiah had predicted regarding the Jewish captivity in Babylon, what did he do? He testified, "I set my face unto the Lord God, to seek by prayer and supplications, *with fasting*, and sackcloth, and ashes" (Daniel 9:3, emphasis added).

When the early church sent out missionaries, how did they do it? "When they had *fasted* and prayed, and laid their hands on them, they sent them away" (Acts 13:3, emphasis added). When those missionaries had to leave their young, struggling churches, soon to be facing "much tribulation," how did they go about it? We are told, "When they had ordained them elders in every church, and had prayed *with fasting*, they commended them to the Lord, on whom they believed" (Acts 14:23, emphasis added). Fasting was a way of life in those days.

Biblical fasting, by the way, is not merely going without food; that would be dieting, not fasting. In the Word of God, fasting is associated with prayer and the idea seems to be that one becomes so burdened in prayer that food loses its appeal. It is never "fasting and prayer," but always "prayer and fasting." Prayer is mentioned first. The intercessor prays right through the lunch hour without being conscious that it is the regular time to eat. And the same is true of the evening or morning meal.

D. He "Prayed!"

Nehemiah not only fasted for four months, he cried continuously to God throughout that same period. "He prayed!" Verse 6 tells us he begged Jehovah to "hear the prayer of thy servant, which I pray before thee now, day and night." It was much more than "now I lay me down to sleep" praying, obviously.

Let me ask, "Do you pray for your church with this kind of burden and concern?" How often and how much do you pray?

Some praying could be described by a product we reported in our *Incidents & Illustrations* column some years back. Called "Saint Sprays" and marketed in 14-ounce cans distributed by a Brooklyn, New York firm, purchasers were to spray the strongly-scented mist while walking around the house and reading aloud the prayer printed on the can. Customers were told to use it as they would candles, holy water, statues and other types of devotions to their favorite saints. An owner of a religious specialty shop in Florida said he had been selling between one and two cans of the spray prayers per week. It is amazing that people could be so asinine and gullible. As Elihu told Job, "Surely God will not hear vanity, neither will the Almighty regard it" (Job 35:13).

Obviously, that kind of prayer isn't going to bring revival to our churches or God's blessing to our homes. The prayer it will take was described in another column about a Green Beret warrior wounded in the battle of Ben Het. Army officials notified the parents of Robert Pryor of their son's condition, informing them the 20-year-old lad was "tottering between life and death."

The Pryors immediately turned to God in fervent intercessory prayer and then, in a desperation born of fear mixed with faith, put a huge sign – 10 feet long and 4 feet high – on the fence in front of their home: **PRAY FOR OUR BOBBY, WOUNDED AT BEN HET**. And pray folks did! *Within three weeks after the prayer vigil started, Army authorities notified the Pryors that Robert was out of danger and making an excellent recovery!*

It was James who reminded us that we "have not, because ye ask not" (James 4:2). One cannot help but wonder what the world would be like if Christians claimed and used the prayer potential as outlined in the Word of God to the fullest extent of God's intention. Surely the "great and mighty things" (Jeremiah 33:3) and the "exceeding abundantly above all that we ask or think" (Ephesians 3:20) would be worth all the time and effort expended to claim the promises.

Prayer is one of the keys to God's blessing and power. Jesus told His disciples, in His sermon on the mount: "Ask, and it shall be given you; seek, and ye shall find; knock, and it shall be opened unto you: for every one that asketh receiveth; and he that seeketh findeth; and to him that knocketh it shall be opened." And James reminded his readers, in addition to what is quoted above, "Ye ask, and receive not, because ye ask amiss, that ye may consume it upon your lusts" (James 4:3).

Nehemiah's weeping, mourning, fasting and praying was evidence of his genuine concern.

Notice next,

II. GENUINE CONFESSION!

The heart of his confession is in verses 6 and 7: *"Let thine ear now be attentive, and thine eyes open, that thou mayest hear the prayer of thy servant, which I pray before thee now, day and night, for the children of Israel thy servants, and confess the sins of the children of Israel, which we have sinned against thee: both I and my father's house have sinned. We have dealt very corruptly against thee, and have not kept the commandments, nor the statues, nor the judgments, which thou commandest thy servant Moses."*

Note that Nehemiah's prayer was personal; he included himself in Israel's sins. If we are going to obtain the ear of God we must admit not only that our churches have failed, but that we, as individuals, have failed. If confession is not personal, it is not genuine. Too many in our day are eager to represent themselves as the Prophet Nathan, shouting to King David, "Thou art the man" (II Samuel 12:7), and too few are willing to join the guilty sinner's response in admitting, "I have sinned against the LORD" (II Samuel 12:13).

Nehemiah included himself, confessing, "I and my father's house have sinned." Perhaps he was referring to the fact that he had stayed in Persia instead of going to Jerusalem with Ezra and the others, although this may not seem logical in the light of what else we know about him. Admittedly, however, it would be easy to understand reluctance to leave a good, comfortable, honored, high-paying position and go to the hardships and deprivations of the people of God in Israel. You might say that, contrary to the actions of Moses, he had chosen to enjoy the pleasures of sin for a season, rather than suffer affliction with the people of God (see Hebrews 11:25). At any rate, he included himself in the confession of Israel's sin, involving himself and making it personal.

It is important that we take notice of what caused his confession, noting exactly what it was based upon. He said in verse 5, "I beseech thee, O LORD God of heaven, the great and terrible God, that keepeth covenant and mercy for them that love him and observe his commandments." Nehemiah was thinking about God's great mercy as he laid his soul bare before Jehovah!

Oh, how we need that attitude in this hour, a fresh vision of the mercy and grace of God in our lives and in our churches! We must see anew the bleeding, broken body of the Son of God, hanging on the accursed cross for us. The more we meditate, the more we will realize – and confess – our sinfulness and failures.

Next, Nehemiah manifested,

III. GENUINE FAITH!

Part of that faith was evidenced when he faced the evil critics who "laughed us to scorn, and despised us, and said, What is this thing that ye do? will ye rebel against the king?" by replying with firm confidence and deep conviction, "The God of heaven, he will prosper us; therefore we his servants will arise and build: but ye have no portion, nor right, nor memorial in Jerusalem" (2:19-20). He not only believed God himself, but he inspired the others at Jerusalem to believe Him, too (2:17-18).

Actually, the ground of Nehemiah's faith was threefold:

A. It Was In God's Word!

With what assurance in prayer he reminded Jehovah, "Remember, I beseech thee, the word that thou commandedst thy servant Moses, saying, If ye transgress, I will scatter you abroad among the nations: but if ye turn unto me, and keep my commandments, and do them; though there were of you cast out unto the uttermost part of the heaven, yet will I gather them from thence, and will bring them unto the place that I have chosen to set my name there" (1:8, 9). He was basing his faith on God's revelation to His people.

He reminded the Lord of some of His promises, such as the ones in Leviticus 26:33-45, Deuteronomy 4:23-31, Deuteronomy 28:63-67, and Deuteronomy 30:1-6. Since God kept His word about scattering Israel, Nehemiah reasoned, He would surely have to keep it about their regathering, their restoration. It is vital to remember, however, that we must keep within the terms of His covenant if we hope to have His help. God's promises are not valid apart from their terms, their conditions.

B. It Was In God's Relation to Them!

Nehemiah expressed it, "Now these are thy servants and thy people ..." (Vs. 10). Since they belonged to Him, it was only right to expect His help, His protection, and His power to be manifested on their behalf.

It is the same with us and our churches today. He has called us His servants, His friends, His people. Even more, we are His children and His heirs! As Romans 8:14-17 expresses it: "For as many as are led by the Spirit of God, they are the sons of God. For ye have not received the spirit of bondage again to fear; but ye have received the Spirit of adoption, whereby we cry, Abba, Father. The Spirit [Himself] beareth witness with our spirit, that we are the children of God; and if children, then heirs; heirs of God, and joint-heirs with Christ; if so be that we suffer with him, that we may be also glorified together."

What a position is ours in Christ! No wonder we have a legitimate and biblical right to expect Him to help us.

C. It Was In God's Power As Experienced in the Past!

Nehemiah went on in verse 10, "... whom thou hast redeemed by thy great power, and by thy strong hand." He has done it before; He can do it again!

In the case of Israel, God's power had delivered them from the bondage and slavery of Egypt. He had delivered them from the Red Sea. He had delivered them again and again during their wilderness wanderings. He had delivered them from the Moabites. He had delivered them from the Philistines. He had delivered them from the Amorites, the Hivites, the Hittites, the Canaanites, the Perizzites, the Jebusites, and all the other "ites" of that day. Surely He could be expected to come through on their behalf one more time – especially if they met the conditions of His Word, which Nehemiah had outlined.

Is it any less with the church of the 21st century? He has delivered us, redeemed us from our sins, made us new creations in Christ – causing old things to pass away and all things to become new – and led us from victory to victory in our Christian lives. As the psalmist expressed it: "He brought me up also out of an horrible pit, out of the miry clay, and set my feet upon a rock, and established my goings. And he hath put a new song in my mouth, even praise unto our God: many shall see it, and fear, and shall trust in the LORD" (40:2, 3).

We are His children, we have His promises in His Word; what more do we need? Nehemiah's faith was built on these three words, outlined on the above: revelation, relation, redemption. That was sufficient for Nehemiah; it should be adequate for us as well.

There is one more thing we need to see, part of Nehemiah's example for us who long for revival and the power of God in our churches today, namely,

IV. GENUINE WORK!

While this theme covers chapters 2 through 6, it is summed up in Nehemiah 4:6, "... the people had a mind to work." They were *willing* to work. They were *united* in work. So the wall was built (6:15).

The need for God's people to be united is a common theme in Scripture. It took Nehemiah and his men being "of one accord" before the walls were rebuilt; it required the Lord's disciples being "of one accord" before the fire fell at Pentecost; it necessitated being "of one accord" before He displayed His power in revival during the march of the Christian church in the centuries since apostolic days. Dear friend, it has always been that way.

That is one reason we should not be surprised over our barrenness and powerlessness today. Our petty differences, our little squabbles, our division into various sects of fundamentalism have held back revival for years. We boast about contending for the faith once delivered when we are really merely promoting our pet views and private theories. *God help us!*

Nehemiah and his fellows worked in spite of opposition. The moment you begin to really work for Him, you will run into all kinds of satanic opposition! Nehemiah and his workers did and so will you.

For one thing, there were **the jeers and sneers of the world**. We are told, "It came to pass, that when Sanballat heard that we builded the wall, he was wroth, and took great indignation, and mocked the Jews. And he spake before his brethren and the army of Samaria, and said, What do these feeble Jews? will they fortify themselves? will they sacrifice? will they make an end in a day? will they revive the stones out of the heaps of the rubbish which are burned? Now Tobiah the Ammonite was by him, and he said, Even that which they build, if a fox go up, he shall even break down their stone wall" (Nehemiah 4:1-3).

What did Nehemiah do? He turned to God in prayer for strength. "Hear, O our God; for we are despised: and turn their reproach upon their own head, and give them for a prey in the land of captivity; and cover not their iniquity, and let not their sin be blotted out from before thee: for they have provoked thee to anger before the builders" (Nehemiah 4:4-5). He and his men didn't let the jeers stop them; they continued to work.

This was followed by **a conspiracy on the part of their enemies** to stop the work. It is summed up in Nehemiah 4:8, "[They] conspired all of them together to come and to fight against Jerusalem, and to hinder it."

What did Nehemiah do? He turned again to God for help, and the very next verse says, "Nevertheless we made our prayer unto our God ...." But that was not all, "... and set a watch against them day and night." As we moderns have expressed it, they trusted the Lord and kept their gunpowder dry; they praised the Lord and passed the ammunition. God will help us in our battles, but He doesn't usually do the fighting for us.

The third opposition came in the form of **discouragement**. The brethren came to Nehemiah and complained, "The strength of the bearers of burdens is decayed, and there is much rubbish; so that we are not able to build the wall. And our adversaries said, They shall not know, neither see, till we come in the midst among them, and slay them, and cause the work to cease" (4:10, 11).

What did Nehemiah do? Once again he leaned upon the Lord to fight with them against their enemies, using the slogan, *"Remember the Lord!"* As Nehemiah 4:14 put it, "I looked, and rose up, and said unto the nobles, and to the rulers, and to the rest of the people, Be not ye afraid of them: remember the Lord, which is great and terrible, and fight for your brethren, your sons, and your daughters, your wives, and your houses."

This was followed by opposition in the form of **internal strife**. Brethren were against brethren, taking advantage of one another in a shameful manner, a story told in Nehemiah 5.

What did Nehemiah do? He did not turn to God with this problem; this was something he could and should handle himself. He "rebuked the nobles" and demanded that the wrongs be made right. Not another stone was put into place in the wall until the matter was settled.

Next came **a proposed compromise** from their enemies. Nehemiah and his men had now finished the wall but not the gates. The problem is told in Nehemiah 6:1-2: "It came to pass, when Sanballat, and Tobiah, and Geshem the Arabian, and the rest of our enemies, heard that I had builded the wall, and that there was no breach left there; (though at that time I had not set up the doors upon the gates;) That Sanballat and Geshem sent unto me, saying, Come, let us meet together in some one of the villages in the plain of Ono. But they thought to do me mischief."

Four times they presented this proposition and four times the answer was negative, "I answered them after the same manner" (Vs. 4). You may recall Pharaoh tried unsuccessfully four times to get Moses to compromise, also.

Thank God, Nehemiah would not let the work cease for any reason whatsoever. The matter is summed up: "I sent messengers unto them, saying, I am doing a great work, so that I cannot come down: why should the work cease, whilst I leave it, and come down to you" (6:3).

He was doing "a great work." I do not speak lightly when I remind you that work for the Lord is the greatest work there is, barring none. Am I *God's man?* Is this *God's work?* Is this *God's way?* Then nothing should stop it; it should never cease for even a single moment!

There is a sense in which Nehemiah could not stop the work. While he could in the physical sense, he couldn't and still be in the will of God, having peace of mind and heart. In this sense he was like Jeremiah, "Then I said, I will not make mention of him nor speak any more in his name. But his word was in mine heart as a burning fire shut up in my bones, and I was weary with forbearing, and I could not stay" (Jeremiah 20:9).

Christians in the 21st century must approach their work in their churches in exactly the same manner, refusing to stop under any circumstances. Yes, *why should the work cease?*

Conclusion

We have looked at Nehemiah's example and applied it to ourselves and to our churches in our day. We readily confess that the job before us is immense, our talents are limited, and our numbers are small. Can we really triumph? Can we actually prevail in this day? Remember, God and one make a majority.

J. Hudson Taylor, the father of modern missions and founder of the China Inland Mission (it celebrated its centennial in 1989) was fond of these three words, proving their progression in his ministry times without number: *impossible, difficult, done.* May it also be true today in your church and mine.

Actually, there are three options, three choices before us:

1. We can sit back, take it easy, and go on in our complacency. That is defeat for us and victory for the enemy.

2. We can mourn, talk, and even plan, but never go any further. That, too, is defeat for us and victory for the enemies of Christ.

3. Like Nehemiah, we can start by weeping, mourning, fasting, praying and confessing our sins, then believe God and go out to the work before us. We can rebuild the walls and restore the gates in Christian experience. That will bring personal victory and triumph for the cause of Jesus Christ.

"The God of heaven, he will prosper us; therefore we his servants will arise and build ..." (2:20).

Chapter 2

THE SHEEP GATE!

*"Then Eliashib the high priest rose up with his brethren the
priests, and they builded the sheep gate; they sanctified it, and
set up the doors of it; even unto the tower of Meah they sanctified it, unto the tower of Hananeel.*

*"And next unto him builded the men of Jericho. And next to
them builded Zaccur the son of Imri."*

– Nehemiah 3:1-2

Cyrus, king of Persia, nearly a century prior to the setting of our
text, had made a proclamation permitting the captive Jews to go back
to Jerusalem. There had been two returns: one almost immediately
under Zerubbabel to rebuild the temple; and one, about 80 years later,
under Ezra for investigation and reformation.

The gates and walls, however, still had not been repaired. Without this
protection, the city had no defense and was continuously in imminent
danger of invasion from her many enemies. Even more embarrassing
and humiliating perhaps, their foes, who formerly feared her so greatly, now openly laughed, despised and mocked the once proud,
impregnable City of Zion.

The opening verses of Nehemiah recorded his personal response
when one of his brethren, Hanani, returned to report that once noble
city's "great affliction and reproach." He had been deeply moved and
his reaction took the form of "weeping, mourning and confessing of
sin" over a period of several months. God intervened and Artaxerxes,
king of Persia at the time, gave Nehemiah permission to return to
Jerusalem and perform whatever repairs were necessary. He also provided him with letters to "the governors beyond the river" and to
Asaph, "the keeper of the king's forest." The first was for *protection*
and the second for *provision*.

This third chapter of Nehemiah records the actual building of the
wall and the gates. In a fashion which would certainly seem strange

to an unbeliever – yea, he would probably call it a fantastic coincidence – but almost commonplace to one who accepts the verbal inspiration of the Word of God, the gates in the order recorded here are symbolic of the major highlights in progressive New Testament Christian experience.

The first one mentioned is the Sheep Gate. Sheep and lambs are mentioned between 450 and 500 times in the Word of God, the first time in Genesis 4:2, when Abel is mentioned as a keeper of sheep and it follows to tell of his offering a lamb as a sacrifice to God (which He accepted, Hebrews 11:4 tells us) although He refused Cain's offering of the fruit of the ground. The last time is in the last chapter of Revelation and features the Lamb of God (22:1-3).

The Sheep Gate is not difficult to identify since it was the one through which animals were led to slaughter on the altar of sacrifice. Our attention is immediately called to the biblical truth that "without shedding of blood is no remission" (Hebrews 9:22), and we are reminded of the One who was "brought as a lamb to the slaughter" (Isaiah 53:7), described by John the Baptist as "the Lamb of God, which taketh away the sin of the world" (John 1:29). To put it in the language of an unknown poet of yesteryear:

> I bend my ear down to the Book, and listen,
>   And back across the centuries I hear
> The tramping of a million little hoofs of lambs
>   To slaughter led.
> As in the night, when I would sleep and dream,
>   I hear them, one by one, approach the place of sacrifice;
> Sweet, gentle, unresistant things,
>   So pure and white.
> And then I turn the Book and hold it near my heart.
>   The little lambs all quiet now, but, oh, I feel
> The even tread of One who walked alone –
>   God's perfect Lamb.
> The footsteps cease – somewhere beyond the city's wall –
>   My heart picks up the surging of a wondrous flow
> That started from His broken heart that day
>   And reached my own.

This gate unmistakably speaks of the Cross of Calvary, of salvation through our Lord Jesus Christ, and of His great atonement. Several considerations force us to this conclusion. For one thing,

I. COMMENCEMENT: *It Was the Starting Point!*

Just as this was the place where Nehemiah and his followers began rebuilding the wall around Jerusalem, so the cross is the starting point for all Christian experience. The sin question must be settled before there can be any Christian life. It is impossible for one to follow the Lord Jesus Christ until he has spiritually passed through this spiritual Sheep Gate.

You can be a church member without coming through this gate, but you cannot be a Christian. You can be a good moral man or woman without passing through this gate – you can even be an active, earnest church worker – but you cannot be a child of God until its symbolism has been personally experienced.

Dear reader, let me gently but earnestly impress upon your heart this vital truth: *you cannot enter into God's heavenly and eternal city until you have passed through this spiritual gate!* I think now of what Jesus said in John 10:9, "I am the door [literally, *the gate*]; by me if any man enter in he shall be saved, and shall go in and out and find pasture." Jesus Christ is not *a* door; He is *the* door, *the gate!* When the Son of God said, "I am the door," He excluded every *one* else and every *thing* else.

The church, although a divine institution playing a vital role in the program of God, is not the door. Faithful preachers of the gospel, even though anointed of God and able through the blessed Word of God and the anointing of the sweet Holy Spirit of God to point their hearers to the door, are not themselves the door. The ordinances of baptism and the Lord's Supper, although given by our Lord and necessary for obedience in the Christian life, are not the door to salvation. Good works, although commanded by God and expected as the norm in every Christian, are not the door. The Law of Moses, even though it must be perfectly fulfilled for salvation to be obtained – and *was* fulfilled by our Representative, Jesus Christ – is not the door.

Let this simple, biblical truth impress your soul: **JESUS CHRIST HIMSELF ALONE IS THE DOOR!** As Simon Peter frankly told the Sanhedrin, "Neither is there salvation in any other: for there is none other name under heaven given among men, whereby we must be saved" (Acts 4:12). And Jesus plainly told His disciples, responding to this very question about the way to Heaven, "I am the way, the truth, and the life, no man cometh unto the Father, but by me" (John 14:6). No words could be plainer, no language more clear. As Jesse Brown Pounds taught us to sing:

> I must needs go home by the way of the Cross,
>   There's no other way but this;
> I shall ne'er get sight of the Gates of Light
>   If the way of the Cross I miss.

Even the significance of the names of the workers at this gate remind us of salvation through Christ. Eliashib, the name of the high priest, means "God will restore." It is only through the death of God's perfect Lamb that a sinner is restored to that fellowship with God which man enjoyed on earth before sin reared its ugly head to besmirch and despoil.

The name of the tower, Meah, is "a hundred"; the *Holman Christian Standard Bible* translates it, "the Tower of the Hundred." At this our thoughts turn immediately to the Lord's parable in Matthew 18:12-14 and Luke 15:1-7, about the man who had 100 sheep and one was lost; how he searched for it until he found it; and then carried it safely on his shoulders to the place of safety.

The name of the other tower, Hananeel, means "to whom God is gracious." It is certainly true that God is gracious to all who pass through the Sheep Gate. Not only so, but His graciousness is abundantly evidenced in even providing such a gate for Hell-deserving sinners in the first place!

The first worker on the other side of the Sheep Gate was Imri's son, Zaccur, which means "well remembered." Evidently this man worked alone, but his name has been preserved in the divine record, God's honor roll of the faithful. You may be sure that all faithfulness to God – all sincere service in His Name – is well remembered now by God, and will be throughout the countless ages of eternity.

Paul put it like this over 2,000 years after Nehemiah, "... forasmuch as ye know that your labor is not in vain in the Lord" (I Corinthians 15:58). And as the Hebrews were promised, "For God is not unrighteous to forget your work and labour of love, which ye have showed toward his name, in that ye have ministered to the saints, and do minister" (Hebrews 6:10).

Other evidence that the Sheep Gate speaks of salvation through the sacrifice of Christ is in the fact,

II. COMPULSION: *It Required the Work of the High Priest!*

Our text says, "Then Eliashib the high priest rose up with his brethren the priests, and they builded the sheep gate; they sanctified it, and set up the doors of it ...." This gate took the sanctified, holy hands of God's high priest to build. In like manner, our great High Priest constructed the Sheep Gate of Christian experience.

He built it *by* and *through* His death on the cross! He built it with His blood, His tears, His agony, with the sacrifice of Himself. Why was He willing to build this gate when it involved such a tremendous personal price? The only answer lies in these three words: *He loved us!* The sweet story is told in John 3:16, "For God so loved the world, that he gave his only begotten Son, that whosoever believeth in him should not perish, but have everlasting life."

Back in the days of the French Revolution there was a prisoner in one of the dungeons who was much beloved by all the people. Both this man and his father were incarcerated in the same penitentiary and both bore the same given name. On one occasion, when it had been announced that several of the inmates were to be executed, the son's name was called along with numerous other ill-favored ones. So great was the father's love for his son, he responded to the call, went to the scaffold, and laid his head on the chopping block. When the blade of the guillotine flashed, his head rolled into the waiting basket. The father died for the son whom he so deeply loved.

In a much grander, nobler manner, that is what Jesus Christ has done for us. We were the guilty, judgment-deserving ones, but He voluntarily took our place and died in our stead, paying in full our penalty, because He loved us. Yes, it took the High Priest's blood to build this gate.

That sacrificial death was not enough, however; He built it also through His resurrection from the tomb. If there had been no resurrection from the dead, there would have been no Sheep Gate, no Christian experience, no Christians in fact. This is a point Paul expressed quite clearly in I Corinthians 15, that great resurrection chapter.

He wrote: *"If Christ be not risen, then is our preaching vain, and your faith is also vain. Yea, and we are found false witnesses of God; because we have testified of God that he raised up Christ: whom he raised not up, if so be that the dead rise not. For if the dead rise not, then is not Christ raised: and if Christ be not raised, your faith is vain; ye are yet in your sins. Then they also which are fallen asleep in Christ are perished. If in this life only we have hope in Christ, we are of all men most miserable. But now is Christ risen from the dead, and become the first-fruits of them that slept"* (Vss. 14-20). Bless His holy Name, we serve a living Savior and not a dead God, One who forever lives to make intercession for us (Hebrews 7:25).

This gate was built with the holy blood of our High Priest. Hebrews 9:11-12, tell us: "But Christ being come an high priest of good things to come, by a greater and more perfect tabernacle, not made with hands, that is to say, not of this building; neither by the blood of goats and calves, but by his own blood he entered in once into the holy place, having obtained eternal redemption for us." This eternal redemption was based completely upon the shed blood of the Lord Jesus Christ, apart from which there would be no Christian experience for anyone.

Because this gate was built with His blood, it can never be destroyed. The physical Sheep Gate in the wall of old Jerusalem was destroyed many times, but the spiritual Sheep Gate built by Christ is eternal. The gates of Hell cannot prevail against it! Because this gate was built with *His* blood, it will never need *re*building.

The Old Testament priests had a continual ministry of sacrifice and bloodshed. The high priest, under the Levitical system, went once a year into the Holy of Holies to sprinkle the blood on the mercy seat and sin was *temporarily* settled thereby for another year. Our High Priest entered on the ground of His own blood once for all, and *eternally* settled the sin question. Hebrews 10:10-14 describes it like this:

"By the which will we are sanctified through the offering of the body of Jesus Christ once for all. And every priest standeth daily ministering and offering oftentimes the same sacrifices, which can never take away sins: but this man, after he had offered one sacrifice for sins for ever, sat down on the right hand of God; from henceforth expecting till his enemies be made his footstool. For by one offering he hath perfected for ever them that are sanctified." Hallelujah!

The Old Testament priests offered only the blood of animals, which could never take away sin (Hebrews 10:4). Christ, on the other hand, had infinite blood. Hence, when He died on the cross, He was able to triumphantly shout, "It is finished!" (John 19:30). *And it is!*

Furthermore, because this gate was built with His sanctified blood, it satisfied every one of the broken laws of justice. Remember that Exodus 34:7, in describing Jehovah God – after talking about His mercy, grace, longsuffering, goodness, truth and forgiveness – added, "that will by no means clear the guilty." God's mercy cannot set aside or nullify His holiness to clear the guilty.

That is why Romans 3 describes Christ's atonement as follows: "Whom God hath set forth to be a propitiation through faith in his blood, to declare his righteousness for the remission of sins that are past, through the forbearance of God; to declare, I say, at this time his righteousness: that he might be just and the justifier of him which believeth in Jesus" (Vss. 25, 26).

The Justifier must be *just* and, apart from Calvary, there was absolutely no other way possible for God to forgive a sinner of his sin and still remain righteous Himself. In the work of the cross God was able to grant forgiveness and still satisfy the demands of holiness and justice. As the poet expressed it,

> 'Tis in the cross of Christ we see
> How God can save, yet righteous be.

Here is another thing about the Sheep Gate:

III. CURING: *It Was a Place Where Disease Was Cured!*

In John 5:1-4, we read: "After this there was a feast of the Jews; and Jesus went up to Jerusalem. Now there is at Jerusalem by the sheep market [lit., *gate*; as in the *Holman Christian Standard Bible* and other translations] a pool, which is called in the Hebrew tongue Bethesda, having five porches. In these lay a great multitude of impotent folk, of blind, halt, withered, waiting for the moving of the water. For an angel went down at a certain season into the pool, and troubled the water: whosoever then first after the troubling of the water stepped in was made whole of whatever disease he had."

So it was at the Sheep Gate that the pool of Bethesda was located. Here men, women and children were healed of whatever diseases they had – no matter whether blind, halt, maimed, lepers, or plagued with some other sickness. It was at this gate, as the passage in John goes on to record, that Christ met and healed the palsied man.

It is significant to note that, although the sick were indeed healed at this gate, it was only through a divine act. It required an angel of God coming down from Glory to trouble the water; the pool itself was unable to cure or heal. And even after the water had been troubled by God's ambassador, only the first one to enter was healed. Not all were healed; only one.

In contrast, think of Christ's spiritual Sheep Gate. Here men are healed of the disease of sin. They, too, are cured by a divine act and that miracle is what the Word of God describes as the new birth. It is not the work of a mere angel, but this redemptive work is by the blessed Holy Spirit of God. John 3:5 says, "Except a man be born of water and of the Spirit, he cannot enter into the kingdom of God." And when the Bible speaks of man's reaction to the Son of God, it says: "But as many as received him, to them gave he power to become the sons of God, even to them that believe on his name: which were born, not of blood, nor of the will of the flesh, nor of the will of man, but of God" (John 1:12-13).

This divine act – the miraculous, regenerating work of the Holy Spirit of God in a new birth experience – takes place the very moment an individual steps through the Sheep Gate by faith, putting his personal faith and trust in the Lord Jesus Christ.

There is one striking difference, however, between the Sheep Gate at Jerusalem and the Sheep Gate provided by Jesus Christ. That difference lies in the Bible truth that *all* who come to Christ in faith are healed! No one is excluded or turned away at this spiritual Sheep Gate. To put it in the words of Christ, "... him that cometh to me I will in no wise cast out"

(John 6:37). Perhaps this is why there is no mention of locks and bars in connection with the Sheep Gate, as is true with most of the other gates in Nehemiah 3. No one is shut out who wishes to enter.

Nor is there a disease of sin His blood won't cure. We think of the liberal clergyman talking to an evangelical woman. Discussing deathbed conversion, he said, "You don't think that deathbed repentance does away with a whole life of sin, do you?"

And she happily retorted, "No, *but Calvary does!*"

The situation still calls for great haste, however, just as with the urgency of seeking to be first into the water at the pool of Bethesda. Today the reason for haste is not in seeking to be first, but because this gate will one day be closed to sinners and opportunity for cleansing will be gone forever. When it is closed, it will never be reopened.

Since this is the only gate for salvation, it behooves us to heed the words of God in II Corinthians 6:2, "... behold, now is the accepted time; behold, now is the day of salvation," and, again, "Today if ye will hear his voice, Harden not your hearts ... lest any of you be hardened through the deceitfulness of sin" (Hebrews 3:7-8, 13).

One other significant matter about the Sheep Gate should be noted,

IV. CLEANSING: *It Was a Place Where Men Were Freed From the Curse!*

Note verse two of our text again, "And next unto him [Eliashib, the high priest] builded the men of Jericho." Here, right along beside the high priest himself, were men who were not Jews; they were foreigners, Gentiles. Even more significant, they were men who had been under the curse of God.

Joshua's conquest of Jericho is a familiar story to all Bible students. After receiving detailed instructions from God about how to gain the victory, Joshua had told the people: "The city shall be accursed, even it, and all that are therein, to the Lord ..." (Joshua 6:17). Even more than that, after the battle had been won, Joshua instructed his followers, "Cursed be the man before the Lord, that riseth up and buildeth this city Jericho: he shall lay the foundation thereof in his firstborn, and in his youngest son shall he set up the gates of it" (Vs. 26).

For hundreds of years no one dared defy Jehovah God on this

matter, until wicked King Ahab and treacherous Queen Jezebel reigned in Israel. At that time Hiel, the Bethelite, rebuilt Jericho. True to the warning of God, "... he laid the foundation thereof in Abiram his firstborn, and set up the gates thereof in his youngest son Segub" (I Kings 16:34). But now, at the Sheep Gate, the name of this city so plagued and cursed by God is identified in a connection with the very high priest of God!

Surely this serves to remind us of the grace of God to be found at the blessed Sheep Gate of Christian experience. The Bible tells us that all men, women and children are under the curse of God because of sin. Galatians 3:10 says, "... for it is written, Cursed is every one that continueth not in all things which are written in the book of the law to do them." In fact, "Whosoever shall keep the whole law, and yet offend in one point, he is guilty of all" (James 2:10). Every one who has ever committed a single sin – *and that includes us all* – is under this terrible curse.

However, just as the men of Jericho were loosed from the curse by yoking up with God's elect earthly people, the Jews, so sinners today can be set free from the curse of sin's condemnation by joining up with God's elect heavenly people, the Christians.

Of course, the only way one can do this is through the new birth, obtained, as already noted, through receiving Jesus Christ as personal Lord and Savior. When one does so, he is set free from the awesome curse of sin and death. That is why Galatians 3:13 says, "Christ hath redeemed us from the curse of the law, being made a curse for us: for it is written, Cursed is every one that hangeth on a tree." Our judgment, our curse, our penalty, fell upon Him as He hung on Calvary's tree, thereby forever freeing us to enter His holy, heavenly city, the New Jerusalem. Thank God, "the blood of Jesus Christ his Son cleanseth us from all sin" (I John 1:7).

One time a young woman lay dying. Apparently her soul was catching visions of the land that is fairer than day for she opened her eyes, looked around her, then raised her right hand and placed her right index finger on the palm of her left hand. Softly and slowly she said, "There – is no – mark – here; but – He – was – wounded – for – my – transgressions."

Dropping her hand, her eyes closed again in an apparent coma.

Then they opened the second time and, looking about her, she raised her right hand to her brow, again saying slowly and softly, "There – are – no – thorns – here; but – He – was – wounded – for – my – transgressions."

Once more her hand dropped to her side, her eyes closed, and there was silence for several minutes. She stirred, her eyes opened the third time, and she put her hand to her side, saying, "There – is – no – spear – here; but – He – was – wounded – for – my – transgressions."

Her hand dropped to the bed again and her eyes closed, but this time her soul took its flight to meet the Maker who had become her Savior. She had learned the precious sweetness of the truth Isaiah proclaimed, "Surely he hath borne our griefs, and carried our sorrows: yet we did esteem him stricken, smitten of God, and afflicted. But he was wounded for our transgressions, he was bruised for our iniquities: the chastisement of our peace was upon him; and with his stripes we are healed. All we like sheep have gone astray; we have turned every one to his own way; and the Lord hath laid on him the iniquity of us all" (Isaiah 53:4-6).

Some time ago I read a story which stirred me deeply – I think in a book of sermons by R. A. Torrey – one that was unusual almost to the point of disbelief.

Many years ago a butcher in a meat packing plant was busy slaughtering lambs. Before him was a lamb securely bound, ready to be killed. He plunged the knife deep into the animal's throat and when the blood spurt out, the little lamb tried to lick with his tongue its own warm blood from the butcher's hand. According to the story, the butcher threw down his knife, took off his apron, and vowed, "I'll never slay, I'll never cut the throat of another lamb again as long as I live."

Yet that is nothing compared with what the Lamb of God has done for you. See Him hanging, bleeding, dying, suffering on the cross of Calvary, rejected by earth, even forsaken by Heaven. See yourself guilty and condemned before God, the very blood of the Lord Jesus staining your rebellious soul as you crucify Him afresh through rejection and indifference. Then realize that even today He stands ready to kiss away the black, bitter guilt with His own precious lips of grace – if only you will repent of your sin and receive Him by faith.

Old-timers may remember Evangelist Walter "Happy Mac"

MacDonald. He held a crusade one time in a church I later pastored in Ohio. Before his conversion he had been a professional entertainer and one time he was in Chicago between engagements. It was back when "Ma and Pa" Taylor were serving as superintendents at the world renowned Pacific Garden Mission, a place where I had the privilege of preaching for a week several years back. Mac, as he was called then, had been drinking heavily and one night he staggered into the mission, became deeply convicted, and returned several nights running. After quite a few nights of intense conviction he had gone to the altar and Ma noticed he was having problems.

She stopped playing the piano (one of two in the mission, gifts of Billy Sunday, who had been saved there when playing ball for the Chicago White Sox) and knelt beside him. He was telling the Lord what a sinner he was and how impossible it would be for God to save the likes of him. Mrs. Taylor began to read and quote Scripture showing the power of Christ in redemption, ending by saying something like, "Mac, Calvary covers it all. Everything you have done will be taken care of by the blood of Christ."

He asked her, with hope now in his voice, to repeat what she had said. Ma said, "Mac, it's true. Calvary covers it all." Light dawned and by faith he claimed the promises of God, saying, "Calvary *does* cover it all! My whole life of sin and shame! Thank you for telling me!"

Mrs. Taylor couldn't get the incident out of her mind and a few days later sat down at the piano and wrote that sweet gospel song, highlighting the chorus Mac's words inspired:

> Calvary covers it all,
> My past with its sin and stain;
> My guilt and despair Jesus took on Him there,
> And Calvary covers it all.

Yes, "God commendeth his love toward us, in that, while we were yet sinners, Christ died for us" (Romans 5:8). This Sheep Gate is for *you!* Have you entered? Thank God, you can begin your Christian life today, one that will never end throughout all the ceaseless ages of eternity.

There is a fountain filled with blood
Drawn from Immanuel's veins;
And sinners, plunged beneath that blood,
Lose all their guilty stains.

The dying thief rejoiced to see
That fountain in his day;
And there may I, though vile as he,
Wash all my sins away

Thank God for the Sheep Gate, the one which allows us to *start* a Christian experience!

Decision for Christ!

Are you a born-again Christian? Have you passed through the Sheep Gate, which speaks of the Lamb of God and His complete atonement at Calvary? Are you trusting Him and Him alone to forgive your sins and save you for eternity?

If not, now that you have read this simple Bible message about the salvation in Christ, this is the time to get the matter settled. Why not stop at once and ask Him to save you, claiming some promise like Romans 10:13, "For whosoever shall call upon the name of the Lord shall be saved"? If you will, write me a letter and tell me of your decision. Or, if you prefer, you may use the form below.

Evangelist Robert L. Sumner
5717 Pine Drive
Raleigh, NC 27606-8947

Dear Brother Sumner:

I have read your sermon, "The Sheep Gate," and realize that I need to trust the Lamb of God, our Lord Jesus Christ, for salvation. Since He has invited all desiring to be saved to come to Him, I come this very moment, trusting Him to both forgive me of my many sins and to give me eternal life, just as He promised in the Bible.

By faith I take Him at His Word, claiming His so great salvation. It is my desire, from this day forward, to live for Him and honor His Word through my actions. Kindly send me a letter of counsel and instruction about how to do this.

(Signed)_____

Address:_____

City:_____

State:_____ Zip _____

Chapter 3

THE FISH GATE

"But the fish gate did the sons of Hassenaah build, who also laid the beams thereof, and set up the doors thereof, the locks thereof, and the bars thereof.

"And next unto them repaired Meremoth the son of Urijah, the son of Koz. And next unto them repaired Meshullam the son of Berechiah, the son of Meshezabeel. And next unto them repaired Zadok the son of Baana.

"And next unto them the Tekoites repaired; but their nobles put not their necks to the work of their Lord."

— Nehemiah 3:3-5

When considering the Fish Gate, probably your thoughts turn automatically to the statements of the Savior, first to Peter and Andrew and then to James and John: "Come ye after me, and I will make you to become fishers of men" (Mark 1:17). If so, you are correct. The Fish Gate is the soul winner's gate in Christian experience, one desperately in need of repair in the lives of most saints today, having been broken down, burned with fire, and for all practical purposes destroyed.

Note that it follows in order immediately after the Sheep Gate experience. It is only natural that some of a new convert's first thoughts after receiving Christ are for his unsaved loved ones and companions. In my own experience, I have found that many times when a sinner asks God to save him, he or she continues in prayer by asking Him to save some loved one or ones. It has not been rare to rise from our knees and have the new convert, face still bathed in tears, say, "Now we've got to get my wife saved" – or a husband, or parents, or another who is on that person's heart. This is a good sign of *real* repentance and *genuine* conversion.

In fact, there are some outstanding illustrations in the Word of God that strongly convince us the Fish Gate immediately follows the Sheep Gate in normal Christian experience.

Just as soon as Andrew had been pointed to the Messiah by John the Baptist, the Scripture relates, "He first findeth his own brother Simon, ... and he brought him to Jesus" (John 1:41-42).

As soon as Philip had been introduced to Christ, he immediately found Nathanael, telling him that the One "of whom Moses in the law, and the prophets, did write" had come (John 1:45). Philip did not have his theology straight yet, being a new convert, but even though he described Jesus as "the son of Joseph," he zealously set out to bring Nathanael to Christ – *and he succeeded!*

When Jesus found the tax collector Levi – or, as he is better known, Matthew – at his place of business and invited him to follow Him, the divine record tells us Matthew "left all, rose up, and followed him" (Luke 5:28). Then the very next verse goes on to tell how Matthew fixed a banquet in his house and invited all his unconverted associates to come to the feast in honor of Jesus.

Matthew later developed spiritually to where God used him to write the first book in the New Testament, but as a new convert he wanted everyone he knew – especially his friends and business associates – to share in the wonderful salvation he had just discovered. It is a natural, normal tendency when one has experienced genuine conversion. If you have found something truly wonderful, you want to share it.

Perhaps the most sensational example of this truth is found in John 4. Jesus won that poor, fallen, harlot woman – married and divorced five times and now living with a man who was not her husband – to Himself at the Sychar well, giving her the water of life. She was so excited that she left her water pot where it was, rushed back to the city, and told everyone, "Come, see a man, which told me all things that ever I did: is not this the Christ?" (Vs. 29).

What happened? "Many of the Samaritans of that city believed on him because of the testimony of the woman" (Vs. 39), and many others went out to meet Christ for themselves ... and then believed on Him (Vs. 42). So many of the townspeople got saved through the witness of this new convert that Jesus used it as an illustration to His disciples of the whitened harvest field, waiting to be reaped (Vss. 35-38).

At this Fish Gate place in Christian experience, it is interesting to note the statement in verse 5 of our text: "And next unto them the Tekoites repaired; but their nobles put not their necks to the work of their Lord." The nobles were apparently too proud to stoop for the hard work in this area. That they were saved people is indicated by the expression, "their Lord," but they would not work at the Fish Gate. Alas, we have a host of 21st century followers of the Tekoites in our evangelical churches at this hour; that is, professing Christians who are too proud to enter wholeheartedly into the work of personal evangelism, those who refuse to fish for men.

Incidentally, of all the ten gates listed in Nehemiah 3, this is the only one where it is specifically stated that anyone *refused* to work! Most pastors will testify that they can get the average members of their churches to do just about anything except fish for men!

However, since this gate speaks of soul winning in our Christian experience, note some vital lessons regarding this greatest of all businesses in the Christian life.

Think with me first about,

I. THE TENDENCY: *Why Should It be Done?*

The simplest answer to the "why" question is this: *because we are commanded to do so by our Lord and Savior!* That sweet passage affectionately referred to as the Great Commission instructs us: "All power is given unto me in heaven and in earth. Go ye therefore, and teach all nations, baptizing them in the name of the Father, and of the Son, and of the Holy Ghost: teaching them to observe all things whatsoever I have commanded you: and, lo, I am with you alway, even unto the end of the world" (Matthew 28:19-20).

The "all nations" admittedly includes India, Africa, China, England, Russia, Japan, Spain, Vietnam, Korea, Rumania, and other world countries – plus all the islands of the sea. But it also includes the United States of America and the community in which you live! The Great Commission is a passage we usually associate in our thinking with people whom we do not know – folks living halfway around the world somewhere. However, it refers just as surely – and every bit as authoritatively – to those with whom we daily come in personal contact as it does to some heathen Hottentot in darkest Africa or some other "mission field."

Actually, the command to evangelize is based upon a biblical necessity. All of mankind is helplessly, hopelessly lost in sin. Unless we reach them with the redemptive gospel of Jesus Christ, they will be doomed and damned in a devil's Hell for all eternity. How urgent is our obligation to throw out the gospel lifeline to these souls drowning in this ocean of lostness!

Back in the days when lighthouses required keepers living there constantly to keep the reflectors shining and clear – and to keep the light consistently burning – a visitor asked a keeper if he were not afraid to stay in such a lonely place, especially during the frequent gales and storms.

The keeper replied, "No, I'm not afraid. We never think of ourselves here."

"Never think of yourself!" exclaimed the visitor. "What do you mean?"

The weather-scarred lighthouse attendant responded, "We know we are perfectly safe. Our only thought here is to have our lamps burning brightly and our reflectors clear so that any who are in danger can be saved."

That is the way it should be with every child of God. While he is perfectly safe, he is a lighthouse placed in a stormy, sinful world by the Savior. If he keeps his life clean and his testimony lamp burning brightly, he may be able to save some who otherwise would be lost for eternity. Since Jesus says to His disciples, "Ye are the light of the world" (Matthew 5:14), it is only fair to ask yourself if you are faithfully, consistently shining for Him so the lost may find their way to the divine port and its eternal safety.

Another reason why every believer should be a fisher of men is found in *the fact that the lost do not seek God; they must be sought*. The heart and mind of every sinner is alienated from God and afar off, Paul told the Ephesians (2:17; 4:18). To the Romans he expressed it this way: "As it is written, There is none righteous, no, not one: there is none that understandeth, there is none that seeketh after God. They are all gone out of the way, they are together become unprofitable; there is none that doeth good, no, not one" (3:10-12). And the familiar text in Isaiah 53:6 says, "All we like sheep have gone astray; we have turned every one to his own way; and the Lord hath laid on him the iniquity of us all."

You see, lost men are running *away* from God, they are taking their *own* way – a path away from Him in rebellion and defiant opposition. It is up to us – you and I who know the truth – to reach them with the saving message of our Lord Jesus Christ before they slip over the precipice of time and out into a lost eternity.

Still another reason why every believer ought to be a soul winner is summed up in *what Christ has done for him*. He left His heavenly home for us, stepping "out of the ivory palaces, into a world of woe."

Try to imagine what this meant for Jesus! He lived, died, was buried, rose again, ascended back into Heaven, and is even now seated at the right hand of God making intercession. If He did all this for us, surely we should be willing to do anything He asks, in loving return out of grateful hearts. One poet put it like this:

> After all He's done for me,
>   After all He's done for me,
> How can I do less
>   Than give Him my best
> And live for Him completely
>   After all He's done for me?

A man in Texas told me how his father in Mississippi, shortly after Lincoln had freed the slaves, went to the defense of a black man. It seems that a white woman had been raped by a Negro and angry neighbors were bent on revenge. They did not know who had committed the foul deed, so they grabbed the first black young man they found and started to hang him from a lower limb on the nearest tree. The father of my friend intervened, refusing to allow the mob to commit the terrible crime. Courageously he defied the angry crowd and, strangely to those who know how mobs normally react, they backed down.

How grateful was that freed Negro! He followed the father of my friend to his plantation, insisting that he be allowed to serve him the rest of his life. And he did, too!

Now if a black man who had been saved from an angry horde – bent on destroying him for a crime he did not commit – felt such devotion to his benefactor, how great should be the response of our hearts to yield fully to the will of the one who has done so much for us in redemption, saving us from spiritual and eternal destruction for sins we have committed! If you agree with Isaac Watts,

> But drops of grief can ne'er repay
> The debt of love I owe:
> Here, Lord, I give myself to Thee –
> 'Tis all that I can do,

then you will need to do the one thing that pleases Him more than anything else: *go after lost sinners for whom He died and seek to win them!* Surely it cost Him more to redeem us than any service on our part will ever cost all of us put together – multiplied by the sands of the seashore.

Another reason why we should make good use of the Fish Gate is because *we never know what the results will be.* No matter how discouraging the outlook, we can never tell how or when God is going to mightily bless our efforts. The one who is, in our mind, the hardest, coldest sinner alive may yield readily to gentle urging. I know that, in my own soul-winning sojourns, some whom I wanted least to visit and witness to – because of the nasty reception I thought I would be given – when I did go were the easiest to win to Christ.

To put it in scriptural language, "In the morning sow thy seed, and in the evening withhold not thine hand: for thou knowest not whether shall prosper, either this or that, or whether they both shall be alike good" (Ecclesiastes 11:6).

It was a stormy Sunday morning in London and even the minister was not able to get to the little Primitive Methodist Chapel for services. One of the laymen looked over the scattered congregation of a dozen or so and thought, perhaps, it might be best to simply dismiss the assembly and go home. Instead, he faithfully conducted a service for the few present, preaching the best he knew how from Isaiah 45:22, "Look unto me, and be ye saved, all the ends of the earth: for I am God, and there is none else." Throughout the message he kept insisting, *"Look and live!"*

That morning a 12-year-old lad "looked and lived," coming to Christ in earnest simplicity. His named was Charles Haddon Spurgeon and he went on to become one of the greatest preachers of the gospel this world has ever known, reaching most of England and London in his day for Christ. His sermons were printed by the ton and sent around the world; in fact, his books are still among the most popular in our day, over a century after his death.

Little did that layman – and we today do not even know his name
– expect such tremendous results from so little effort at a time of such
unseemly conditions. No, we never know what the results will be and
for that very reason we are always to be faithful in getting out the
gospel of Christ Jesus through every means available.

One other reason I must mention for evangelizing is wrapped up
in the Bible truth that *there really is a Heaven and there really is a
Hell*. A sweet, beautiful Heaven awaits the redeemed, a wonderful
country where there will be no tears, death, night, pain, sorrow or crying. This land that is fairer than day is an exclusive residence. None
but the ones who have been born of the Spirit of God will ever enter
that lovely paradise.

On the other hand, there is also a hot, horrible Hell of torment for
every unbeliever. Our Lord warned: "And fear not them which kill
the body, but are not able to kill the soul: but rather fear him which is
able to destroy both soul and body in hell" (Matthew 10:28). He said
again, "Ye serpents, ye generation of vipers, how can ye escape the
damnation of hell?" (Matthew 23:33).

Does someone question, "What is the exact nature of Hell?"

We do not know, precisely. The awful judgment of God in pouring
brimstone and fire upon Sodom, Gomorrah and the other cities of the
plain in Genesis 19 offers just a small clue. Jude 7 says, "Even as
Sodom and Gomorrha, and the cities about them in like manner, giving themselves over to fornication, and going after strange flesh, are
set forth for an example, suffering the vengeance of eternal fire." And
in II Peter 2:6, we read, "Turning the cities of Sodom and Gomorrha
into ashes condemned them with an overthrow, making them an
ensample unto those that after should live ungodly."

If you could visualize the awful suffering and agony experienced
by the sinners of Sodom, then perhaps you would be able to visualize
just a small portion of the agony and torment awaiting the individual
who dies in his sin, outside of the shelter in Jesus Christ.

Jesus was emphasizing the horribleness of Hell when He described
it in these terms: *"And if thy hand offend thee, cut it off: it is better
for thee to enter into life maimed, than having two hands to go into
hell, into the fire that never shall be quenched: Where their worm*

dieth not, and the fire is not quenched. And if thy foot offend thee, cut it off: it is better for thee to enter halt into life, than having two feet to be cast into hell, into the fire that never shall be quenched: Where their worm dieth not, and the fire is not quenched. And if thine eye offend thee, pluck it out: it is better for thee to enter into the kingdom of God with one eye, than having two eyes to be cast into hell fire: Where their worm dieth not, and the fire is not quenched." (Mark 9:43-48).

How can anyone who claims to believe that the Bible is the inspired Word of the Living God refuse to work day and night in this business of trying to keep people out of such a horrible Hell?

Years ago, a vile criminal in England was apprehended for his unlawful deeds. Tried and found guilty, he was sentenced to die by hanging. Minister after minister sought to go to his cell to see him before he died, but one by one he refused them admittance to his quarters.

Eventually, however, one did get into his cell and started to explain the simplicity of salvation. He used all the arguments at his disposal in an attempt to break down the obvious hardness of the man's heart and win him for Christ. Execution was only hours away.

When the condemned criminal displayed nothing but utter indifference, the minister finally exclaimed, "Man, don't you realize that in a few hours your life will be taken and your soul will be hurled into another world?"

"Yes," he replied, "as to the fact of my life being taken, I am well aware of that grim truth. But as to my soul going into another world, I have no idea whether that is true or false."

When the minister attempted to deal with him further, the prisoner simply stood to his feet and exclaimed with great emotion, "Sir, if I believed what you say is true, that a man outside of Christ who dies in his sins will be in a burning Hell forever, if I believed that – and had opportunity to do so – I would crawl on my hands and knees to every individual possible in England and beg him to turn to God before it was too late." That is a sobering thought, is it not?

The story of this incident so moved C. T. Studd, son of a wealthy planter in England converted under D. L. Moody, that he volunteered for missions and became involved as a student with six others in the illustrious group known as "the Cambridge Seven," eventually going to China and giving away his fortune to evangelistic causes – later working in America, South India and Africa. In spite of poor health that forced him home from the field several times, he founded such lasting works as the Volunteer Student Missionary Union and the Heart of Africa Mission, which later became the Worldwide Evangelization Crusade.

I wonder if we really do believe what God has said about the flaming fires of Hell? Could we eat our three meals a day and sleep our eight or nine hours a night if we were really convinced our husband, or our wife, or our children, or other loved ones and friends are just a heartbeat's failure from an eternal Hell? How it behooves us to get busy fishing for the souls of men.

Before we leave the reasons for fishing for men, perhaps we should note that *nothing else works* when it comes to fulfilling the Great Commission. Nearly two decades ago I was covering for our magazine a large convention. One speaker, preaching on Psalm 126:6 ("He that goeth forth and weepeth, bearing precious seed, shall doubtless come again with rejoicing, bringing his sheaves with him"), declared, "Someone has said that the average Christian has heard 4,000-5,000 sermons, 8,000-10,000 public prayers, and has sung as many as 20,000 hymns and *led no one to Jesus Christ!* The needs of our land and of our people are too great for us to continue at this pace." And he concluded, "There is a better way and it's outlined for us in verse 6." And so it is!

Consider next, about work at the Fish Gate,

II. THE TECHNIQUE: *How Should It Be Done?*

Let me answer first by saying that fishing for men should always be done through *prayer and the guidance of the blessed Holy Spirit of God.* Surely all agree that we need His guidance, His direction, His enabling for this spiritual work. But it is equally true that prayer is the key for receiving these essentials from Him.

Lack of prayer means lack of power. Many a zealous soul winner's failure can be traced back to a lack of earnest waiting on God before launching his assault into the enemy territory in a battle for the sinner's soul.

The familiar story of the marble cutter is most applicable here. When a minister watched him, chisel and hammer in hand, changing a stone into a beautiful statue, the clergyman lamented, "I wish I could get that kind of result on stony hearts."

The workman stopped, thought a minute, looked the preacher straight in the eye, and said, "Perhaps you could, if you worked as I do, *on your knees!*"

Right there is the key to successful soul winning!

Another way that fishing for men can be done is through the *Christian life and example.* It is still true that what we are speaks so loudly others cannot hear what we say. If we are to succeed for God in fishing for men, our deeds and our actions must harmonize with our words. Second Corinthians 6:3 warns "workers together with him" that they should be "giving no offence in any thing, that the ministry be not blamed."

We should give no affront in anything; that is, put no obstruction in anyone's way that would cause him or her to stumble; being careful that no fault can be found and our ministry blamed or discredited. In other words, we are to give no one any excuse for refusing the Savior because of our actions, our example before them.

In one church, after a great spiritual awakening which had ushered many into the kingdom of God, one man rose in a testimony session to tell what had influenced him to surrender to Christ. It seems that six months previously he had selected one of the prominent members to scrutinize. He had watched his life closely, not only in church but in business and society as well. He not only personally observed all he could, but he made inquiry from others about the man's life.

After six months of such microscopic scrutiny, he testified: "I thank God for that man. He stood the test. I was so convinced of the genuineness of his faith that I, too, received Jesus Christ as my own personal Savior."

I wonder how many would be convinced of their need of salvation by examining your life or mine for six months? Are we consistently living for the Lord Jesus Christ? That is a very real part of fishing for men, what I call the *real* lifestyle evangelism. If our walk fails to match our talk – if our manner of life doesn't live up to our message – all of our testifying, personal work, visitation, and other forms of evangelism will only hinder the cause, not help.

There is no room at the Fish Gate for those who parrot, "Do as I say, not as I do." You must practice what you preach to be successful in this form of fishing!

Another way that fishing for men should be done is through *word of mouth*. Occasionally you will hear a Christian say, "I do not witness with my lips. I let my life do my witnessing for me." While that sounds very pious – especially in the light of what we just discussed – the obvious truth of the matter is that a silent witness cannot do anywhere near the job a verbal one does. The silent Christian – called "undercover Christians" by some – no matter how clean living, will not have anywhere near the souls to lay at the Master's feet as does one who uses his lips to beg others to turn from sin unto salvation.

It is amazing how many pious, clean-living Christians never warn one single lost person or try to win him to Christ. A few years ago, during a meeting in a Midwestern city, the pastor and I called on an elderly couple who lived almost across the street from the church. They very cordially received us at the door and we went into the home, took a proffered seat, and began conversing with them.

Neither was able to get out to our services, I soon discovered, because of age and adverse physical conditions. Almost as soon as we started talking, I also learned that for a full decade the husband had served as custodian in another church in that city, one which had a national and international reputation for its orthodoxy and fundamentalism.

Telling him I thought that was wonderful, I inquired as to when he had gotten saved. Imagine my surprise and chagrin to learn from his own lips that he had never trusted Christ! Further pressing revealed that, in the decade he had worked at that citadel of fundamentalism, not one person had ever, one single time, spoken to him about the Lord Jesus Christ and his relationship to Him.

That great church had experienced scores of Bible conferences, revival crusades, missionary conferences, and a steady stream of outstanding international pulpiteers on its platform. Yet not one missionary, or evangelist, or visiting pastor, or deep Bible teacher had ever concerned himself enough about the janitor to inquire about his soul. At least three mighty men of God served that pulpit as pastor during the time this man was the custodian – if I were to reveal their names you would be shocked – yet not one of the three took time to try to win him to Christ! These "busy" pastors had so much to do with their various programs that the precious fish God had placed in their pond went unnoticed and uncaught.

Perhaps all the visiting speakers thought the custodian in such a great church would be a Christian, I do not know. It certainly taught me a lesson! I have never taken for granted a janitor's salvation since that time and I make it a policy to personally ascertain the spiritual condition of the custodian wherever I go.

This man told me that when the church hired him it was with the understanding that they wanted a custodian who was not a member of the church. It seems that a problem arose with a previous janitor who had been a member, and they decided the new man should be a non-member. But it seems too bad that they were willing to let a man go to Hell just because they didn't want their employee to be a member of the congregation – a rule not directed in that church at secretaries or other staff members, by the way.

Incidentally, the custodian's wife had gone to church there every Sunday morning, but she sat in the large empty auditorium during the Sunday school hour because she did not feel welcome in any of the adult classes – a fact fairly obvious since no one had ever invited her to join them. Thank God, I was able to win them both to Christ that day!

Before we leave this question about how soul winning should be done, let me say that there is no limit to the list. You can invite people to church and you can personally bring them. You can be a soul winner through writing letters, distributing tracts, even by giving your pastor names of unconverted friends, relatives and neighbors. Yes, the list is endless.

Of the people saved in church, I suppose the overwhelming majority of them are brought in by someone other than the preacher. How we need to follow the theme Alexcenah Thomas, back in the 1800s, taught Christians to sing:

> Bring them in, bring them in,
>   Bring them in from the fields of sin;
> Bring them in, bring them in,
>   Bring the wand'ring ones to Jesus.

What a thrill, what a joy to see someone you brought to the service step out and claim Christ openly! And may I remind you that it takes no eloquent tongue, no pleasing personality, to write letters or distribute gospel tracts. *Anyone* and *everyone* can do it.

Remember, too, "So shall my word be that goeth forth out of my mouth: it shall not return unto me void, but it shall accomplish that which I please, and it shall prosper in the thing whereto I sent it" (Isaiah 55:11). While this verse refers to prophecy made by Almighty God being fulfilled, there is a secondary application relating to giving out His Word in ministry, both from the pulpit and in personal soul winning.

Consider with me one more matter regarding our Fish Gate ministry, namely,

III. THE TIME: *When Should It Be Done?*

This can be summed up in one word: **NOW!**

The longer we delay, the more difficult it becomes. If you take a vessel fresh from the potter's wheel, the pressure of a finger will dent it. However, after that vessel has been put through the fire, no pressure of the hand – no matter how great – will affect it. It can be broken, but it cannot be reshaped.

That is the way it is with the hearts of sinners. When they are young, they are soft, pliable and easily molded. But as Hebrews 3:13 teaches, hearts become "hardened through the deceitfulness of sin" and the longer we put off speaking, the less pliable we will find them. We often talk about the sinful, wicked, neglecting *sinners*, but the truth of the matter is that the neglect of indifferent *saints* to speak to them is just as sinful and just as wicked.

Further, if we delay too long, some souls will suddenly step into a lost eternity and their blood will be upon our hands. It will be our responsibility that they died unconverted, and we will personally answer to God about it. As Jehovah said to Ezekiel, "If the watchman see the sword come, and blow not the trumpet, and the people be not warned; if the sword come, and take any person from among them, he is taken away in his iniquity; but his blood will I require at the watchman's hand" (33:6).

You and I who know Christ are God's watchmen; we are responsible for blowing the gospel trumpet and warning sinners of coming judgment. If the Holy Spirit speaks to us about witnessing to some soul and we fail, God tells us: "When I say unto the wicked, O wicked man, thou shalt surely die; if thou dost not speak to warn the wicked from his way, that wicked man shall die in his iniquity; but his blood will I require at thine hand" (Ezekiel 33:8).

Oh, dear brothers and sisters in Christ, the time is short. *It is later than you think!* Death may call us or claim us at any moment. None has any assurance of the next short breath.

Remember, too, our Lord's promise, "Surely I come quickly" (Revelation 22:20).

Will Jesus Christ be satisfied with the number of souls you will have to present to Him when He comes? Or will you be "ashamed before him at his coming" (I John 2:28)?

The unknown poet expressed my own sentiments exactly when he penned,

> And when in the mansions above,
>   The saved all around me appear;
> I want to hear somebody say,
>   'It was you who invited me here'!

When I was a young preacher, just starting out in the ministry, I ran across a bulletin published by the Banker's Life Insurance Company for its agents. It said:

> "WHEN your first morning thought is how you can reach and sell your first prospect –
> "WHEN you hurry through breakfast so you can be started on your way to actual operations –
> "WHEN you can withstand the temptation to pour over the box scores on the sporting page –
> "WHEN you shake off spring fever and snap right up to one prospect after another, fresh and strong for each encounter –
> "WHEN you can keep the corners of your mouth up and wear a smile in the face of successive defeats –
> "WHEN you can eat a little lunch, pass up the noon movies, avoid a little game of pool, or friendly rummy –

"WHEN you can step right back into the fight at 1 p.m. and carry right on to the finish of the business day –

"WHEN you can give up parties and theaters at night to go out and get them where they live –

"WHEN you can devote your last waking thoughts to ideas for your work and plans for business-getting the next day –

"WHEN you can breathe, eat, sleep, think, and permeate your whole life with nothing but life insurance –

"THEN you will be giving up many fancies and pleasures, and much ease and freedom –

"BUT SAY!! YOU WILL BE A BIG SUCCESS IN YOUR BUSINESS!"

I remember how that stirred me when I read it! Should I, as a minister of the gospel of our Lord Jesus Christ – or simply as a Christian – do any less in my service for Jesus Christ and in my efforts to win others to Him, than a life insurance salesman who has a totally materialistic motive and philosophy? *Can* we, *should* we, *dare* we give God any less? Should a life insurance agent have any more devotion to his company than a Christian to his Redeemer?

Never!

What are you doing, dear friend, for souls? Where do you stand in relation to the Fish Gate in your Christian experience? Have you passed through the Sheep Gate, but gone no further?

> O Church of Christ, what wilt thou say
> When in that awful judgment day
> They charge thee with their doom?

The Word of God says: "He that withholdeth corn, the people shall curse him: but blessing shall be upon the head of him that selleth it .... The fruit of the righteous is a tree of life; and he that winneth souls is wise" (Proverbs 11:26, 30).

Or, literally, "He that is wise winneth souls."

How wise are you?

Chapter 4

THE OLD GATE

"Moreover the old gate repaired Jehoiada the son of Paseah, and Meshullam the son of Besodeiah; they laid the beams thereof, and set up the doors thereof, and the locks thereof, and the bars thereof.

"And next unto them repaired Melatiah the Gibeonite, and Jadon the Meronothite, the men of Gibeon, and of Mizpah, unto the throne of the governor on this side the river.

"Next unto him repaired Uzziel the son of Harhaiah, of the goldsmiths. Next unto him also repaired Hananiah the son of one of the apothecaries, and they fortified Jerusalem unto the broad wall.

"And next unto them repaired Rephaiah the son of Hur, the ruler of the half part of Jerusalem.

"And next unto them repaired Jedaiah the son of Harumaph, even over against his house. And next unto him repaired Hattush the son of Hashabniah.

"Malchijah the son of Harim, and Hashub the son of Pahathmoab, repaired the other piece, and the tower of the furnaces.

"And next unto him repaired Shallum the son of Halohesh, the ruler of the half part of Jerusalem, he and his daughters."

– Nehemiah 3:6-12

Of the 10 gates in Nehemiah 3, this is probably one of the most difficult to classify. Yet we think the most obvious answer lies in Jehovah's appeal to His people through the weeping prophet: "Thus saith the LORD, Stand ye in the ways, and see, and **ask for the old paths**, where is the good way, and walk therein, and ye shall find rest for your souls. But they said, We will not walk therein" (Jeremiah 6:16, emphasis added).

This is the place in Christian experience where you "chart your course," and Jehovah's appeal is for those who name His Name to choose "the old paths."

This is also, Jeremiah said, the "good way." It is not necessarily the *easy* way. There may be many trials, tribulations, testings, hardships, persecutions, and oppositions – possibly even martyrdom – to face by those who travel this highway. The "old paths" may lead to a den of lions, as it did for Daniel; or a fiery furnace, as it did for the three Hebrew children; or a dungeon, as it did for Paul and Silas; or a chopping block, as it did for John the Baptist and the Apostle James.

Traveling this thoroughfare means there will be a roaring lion to face as an adversary, one who seeks to battle and conquer. Peter tells us, "Be sober, be vigilant; because your adversary the devil, as a roaring lion, walketh about, seeking whom he may devour" (I Peter 5:8).

There are spiritual mountains to climb on this old highway, some of which might be likened to the Mount Everest or Mount St. Helens variety. There are raging rivers to cross, deep valleys of trouble and sorrow to pass through, and, for some, it may mean the loss of friends, or finances, or loved ones.

As G. A. Young expressed it:

> Some thro' the waters, some thro' the flood,
> Some thro' the fire, but all thro' the blood;
> Some thro' great sorrow, but God gives a song,
> In the night season and all the day long.

This does not keep it from being the "good way," however, and whatever opposition is encountered is always in the light of Isaiah 43:2, where our Lord promised, "When thou passest through the waters, I will be with thee; and through the rivers, they shall not overflow thee: when thou walkest through the fire, thou shalt not be burned; neither shall the flame kindle upon thee."

Paul, who was perhaps tried by the testing fire more than any other single mortal in the history of mankind (see II Corinthians 11:16-31), confessed triumphantly, *"Notwithstanding the Lord stood with me, and strengthened me; that by me the preaching might be fully known, and that all the Gentiles might hear: and I was delivered out of the mouth of the lion. And the Lord shall deliver me from every evil work, and will preserve me unto his heavenly kingdom: to whom the glory for ever and ever. Amen"* (II Timothy 4:17-18).

No, this highway is not necessarily the easy way, nor is it the *popular* way. It is definitely not the way of the world, the path pursued by the crowd. Matthew 7:13-14, sum it up: "Enter ye in at the straight gate: for wide is the gate, and broad is the way, that leadeth to destruction, and many there be which go in thereat: because straight is the gate, and narrow is the way, which leadeth unto life, and few there be that find it." This is the highway where "few" sojourners are found; the "many" have chosen, instead, the broad road of sin and destruction.

But while this good way is neither the easy way nor the popular way, it is the way where *"ye shall find rest for your souls."* Weary, sin-sick, discouraged, downtrodden individuals by the millions have come to travel this highway, joyously discovering that it fulfills the words of Christ in His great invitation: "Come unto me, all ye that labour and are heavy laden, and I will give you rest. Take my yoke upon you, and learn of me; for I am meek and lowly in heart: and ye shall find rest unto your souls. For my yoke is easy, and my burden is light" (Matthew 11:28-30).

The venerable J. C. Ryle, known and loved for his 6-volume *Expository Thoughts on the Gospels*, also published a volume in 1878 he titled *Old Paths*. In his Preface he explained its contents: *"It contains nothing but the 'Old Paths' in which the Apostolic Christians, the Reformers, the best English Churchmen for the last three hundred years, and the best Evangelical Christians of the present day, have persistently walked. From these 'paths' I see no reason to depart. They are often sneered at and ridiculed, as old-fashioned, effete, worn out, and powerless in the Nineteenth Century. Be it so. 'None of these things move me.' I have yet to learn that there is any system of religious teaching, by whatever name it may be called, High, or Broad, or Romish, or Neologian, which produces one quarter of the effect on human nature that is produced by the old, despised system of doctrine which is commonly called Evangelical ... The longer I live the more I am convinced that the way of the school to which I belong is the 'more excellent way.' The longer I live the more I am convinced that the world needs no new Gospel, as some profess to think. I am thoroughly persuaded that the world needs nothing but a bold, full unflinching teaching of the 'old paths'."* I agree totally and completely today with what this old master wrote nearly a century and a third ago.

Recently I read an editorial on a New Year and the writer spoke of how he enjoyed taking new roads. It was pertinent and timely for that occasion. However, when it comes to matters of doctrine, only the "old roads" will do.

Perhaps one of the most important things about the old way, the faith of our fathers, is what the classic gospel song, written by an unknown poet, had to say in the final two verses of "The Old-Time Religion:"

> It will do when I am dying,
>   It will do when I am dying,
> It will do when I am dying,
>   And it's good enough for me.

> It will take us all to Heaven,
>   It will take us all to Heaven,
> It will take us all to Heaven,
>   And it's good enough for me.

God wants His people, those who have experienced the conversion of the Sheep Gate and are filled with the enthusiasm of winning others at the Fish Gate, to chart their course in His 'old' paths. Remember that Malachi 3:6 quotes Him, "I am the LORD, I change not," and Hebrews 13:8 speaks of "Jesus Christ the same yesterday, and to day, and for ever." Since God is the same, since He never changes, since He is eternal, then surely His order, His way, is everlasting also. As the hymn writer, George H. Carr, expressed it,

> The Old Book and the Old Faith
>   Are the Rock on which I stand!
> The Old Book and the Old Faith
>   Are the bulwark of the land!
> Thro' storm and stress they stand the test,
>   In ev'ry clime and nation blest;
> The Old Book and the Old Faith
>   Are the hope of ev'ry land!

Now, as in Nehemiah's day, this gate is torn down and burned with fire across our land – and around the world. Truly we need to return to the way of the Sacred Scriptures, the Holy Bible – to come back to *the God of our fathers* in a personal, intimate relationship, and to *the faith of our fathers* in our daily living.

Let us ask and answer some timely questions along this line. First,

I. THE PROPOSITION: *Why We Need to*
Stick to the "Old Paths"

One reason is that sin and its bitter consequences have not changed. There has been no 21st century repeal of Numbers 32:23, "Be sure your sin will find you out," or of Galatians 6:7, "Be not deceived; God is not mocked: for whatsoever a man soweth, that shall he also reap."

The fools sin made 6,000 years ago were no bigger than the ones sin is making at the present hour. Today's experience agrees with the observation of Eliphaz, "Even as I have seen, they that plow iniquity, and sow wickedness, reap the same" (Job 4:8).

Furthermore, righteousness and its values have not changed. It still pays to do right; living for Jesus still produces big and lasting dividends. The man who does right and lives a dedicated, consecrated life for the Lord Jesus Christ is still far ahead of the one who doesn't.

Mrs. C. D. Martin wrote about a century ago:

> They call me old-fashioned because I believe
>   That the Bible is God's Holy Word,
> That Jesus, who lived among men long ago,
>   Is divine, and the Christ of God.
>
> Old-fashioned because I believe and accept
>   Only what has been spoken from Heav'n;
> Old-fashioned because at the cross I was saved,
>   At the cross had my sins forgiv'n.
>
> Old-fashioned, because I am bound to do right,
>   To walk in the straight narrow way;
> Because I have given my whole life to God,
>   Old-fashioned, because I pray.
> Old-fashioned because I am looking above
>   To Jesus, my glorified Lord;
> Because I believe He is coming again,
>   Fulfilling His holy Word.

And then the impressive chorus:

> My sin was old-fashioned, My guilt was old-fashioned,
> God's love was old-fashioned, I know;
> And the way I was saved was the old-fashioned way,
> Through the blood that makes whiter than snow.

Think with me again,

II. THE PLACE: *Where Does This Old Gate Need Repairing?*

A. In Our Country!

Desperately, the Old Gate needs a complete overhaul in our nation. Uncle Sam must occupy his place at the mourners' bench if America is to be spared the judgment of God's wrath. How applicable for our own land are the old-time warnings of God: "Righteousness exalteth a nation: but sin is a reproach to any people" (Proverbs 14:34), and, "The wicked shall be turned into hell, and all the nations that forget God" (Psalm 9:17). The statement in Proverbs 28:13 is just as true of nations as it is individuals, "He that covereth his sins shall not prosper: but whoso confesseth and forsaketh them shall have mercy."

Soloists can stand and loudly sing "God Bless America" until their throats become raw and sore, but God *cannot* and *will not* bless America until America blesses God. We need revival, reformation and restoration to sweep in Holy Spirit power across this country in each of our 50 States and the District of Columbia – *especially in our nation's capital!*

I think it is highly significant that the co-rulers of Jerusalem are mentioned as working here at the Old Gate. Verse 9 tells us, "And next unto them repaired Rephaiah the son of Hur, the ruler of the half part of Jerusalem." Then in verse 12, "And next unto him repaired Shallum the son of Halohesh, the ruler of the half part of Jerusalem, he and his daughters." Also, verse 7 speaks of "the throne of the governor." And in this group of workers was Malchijah (Vs. 11), whose name means "Jehovah's King."

How desperately our nation needs spiritual men in places of leadership on all levels of government: national, state and local. The Old Gate truly needs repairing all across our country.

We need to rebuild the old-fashioned standards of *morality* and *decency.* Adultery is becoming as popular in this country as soap operas with women and football with men. In the 1970 United States census, there were 523,000 "unmarried couples" in America living together. But the latest figures we have (the 2000 census) – presented in the Census Bureau's Marital Status and Living Arrangements charts, which assures us its figures are "the most recent, most accurate statistics available" – show 9.7 million Americans living with an unmarried 'different sex' partner, plus 1.2 million living with a 'same-sex' partner. In short, the number of openly defiant adulterous sinners in our nation has increased 20-fold in the last third of a century. The tragic thing, speaking strictly as a patriot, is that few seem to think this is bad!

To add to the tragedy of consensual sex sin, according to the National Sexual Assault Hotline, a sexual assault takes place every 154 seconds in this country, approximately one every 2 minutes – and the ratio is going down, probably because rape is becoming more and more unnecessary in our "liberated" society. Why take by force what is offered willingly? What *is* increasing is date rape, thanks to such convenient and available drugs as GHB (gamma hydrobutynic acid), Rohpnol (flunitrazepan), and Ketamine (ketamine hydrochloride).

As a matter of fact, our government is officially encouraging sin through its Department of Health, Education and Welfare. That agency published a pamphlet, "Unmarried Parents – a Guide for the Development of Services in Public Welfare." While not all the children of unmarried parents are illegitimate, of course, the theme seems to be that sin pays and that its penalties, at least in this country, have been repealed. *Christian Economics* summed up the teaching of the pamphlet as follows:

> Welfare workers are instructed to make no mention of religion or moral principles; they are warned against any thought of judgmental attitude; no one is to be made to feel guilty because of wrongdoing; there is to be no penalty and no punitive attitude; no one is to be made to feel any sense of remorse for wrongdoing; care is to be provided for illegitimate children and their mothers, **superior to that which any mother who respects society can afford;** illegitimate paternity is no longer to be a criminal offense; need alone qualifies one for relief; taxpayers' interest in saving money is not to

be considered, all roadblocks to certifying new cases are to be set up and in general welfare services are to be made easier and more generous.

Note the systematic discouragement to all ideas of morality and the eagerness with which the Department is seeking new clients. Note the absence of all sense of right and wrong, of all thought of repentance, restitution and reform.

The Bible tells us that the basis of restoring the sinner to loving acceptance in the community is repentance, restitution, insofar as possible, and reform. The welfare state denies the necessity for a change of heart, defies the law of God in this respect and enables the sinner to live from the labor of others in further defiance of God's command (emphasis added).

This same idea of trying to make sin respectable was highlighted in a message by Dr. G. B. Chisholm, renowned psychiatrist and former head of the United Nations' World Health Organization, who sneered at the idea of sin. He boldly asserted: "For many generations we have bowed our necks to the yoke of the conviction of sin. We have swallowed all manner of poisonous certainties fed us by our parents, our Sunday school teachers, our politicians, our priests, our newspapers, with the best interest in controlling us." Those who believe like Chisholm are increasing on every hand, and growing in places and positions of authority.

Out in California, the State Supreme Court ruled that unwed love is not a crime. That decision stated that California cities and counties have no power to regulate anyone's sex life and that any local ordinance making fornication or isolated acts of adultery a crime are illegal and void. The court's opinion was made in a case involving a woman by the name of Carol Lane – who had been twice convicted of violating a "resorting" ordinance enacted by the Los Angeles city council prohibiting anyone from using "any vacant lot, room, rooming house, lodging house, residence, apartment house, motel ... for the purpose of having sexual intercourse with a person to whom he or she is not married."

A total of 1,415,995 unmarried women gave births in the last year for which we could find figures (2003). In fact, 34.6% of all the babies born in America were illegitimate. Only God keeps records on the number of "shotgun weddings" that keep this ratio down – as do wicked, evil, murderous abortions.

So what should we say about this slaughter of the innocent, the approximately 1,500,000 precious babies murdered annually – the estimated 47th million victim abortionists themselves estimate was killed in 2005? It reached 1,588,600 in 1979 and remained constant for several years, although now it is dropping, probably because so much more is learned about this evil practice. Some of our statistics were gleaned from the Center for Disease Control, whose records have been documented as being very pro-abortion biased (admittedly, we didn't even know being pregnant was a 'disease' until we read CDC's materials), but abortion is a form of legalized killing no matter how you slice it.

While at one time the baby massacre in this country was around 1,600,000 annually, if we limit the average to a conservative 1,400,000 figure for the 34 years since the 1973 Roe v. Wade Supreme Court decision, that is the murder of some 47,600,000 babies who had every right to "life, liberty and the pursuit of happiness," but were selfishly denied that opportunity by mothers who put their own whims and desires ahead of the children they *personally* conceived. That number is equal to one-sixth or one-seventh the present population of the country. And it is a number that *exceeds* the population of many nations.

Baptists For Life once put it like this: "On an average day in this country, 3 times as many babies are killed by their mothers as both men and women die of cancer! In fact, on such a day 8,331 people die, but of that number 3,231 are murdered by their mothers via abortion."

Actually, the evil snake of abortion has slithered into our evangelical churches. Randy Alcorn, in his *Does The Birth Control Pill Cause Abortions,* quotes the latest Alan Guttmacher Institute study as saying "nearly one out of five women getting surgical abortions claims to be a born again Christian." That is a shocking, tragic revelation. Alcorn also quoted a Kaiser Family Foundation survey as finding that "many doctors who would not perform surgical abortions would prescribe the abortion pill, RU-486." Is abortion the death of a child? If so, what difference does it make how the murder is executed, by knife or by pill?

America has also forgotten the biblical dictum, "What therefore

God hath joined together, let not man put asunder" (Mark 10:9), and divorce in America is becoming as common as crab grass on Houston lawns in August. Back in 1910 the ratio was only 1 divorce in 11 marriages and as recently as 1960 it was 1 in 4. In 1986 it was about 1 in 2, a total of 1,159,000 divorces against 2,400,000 marriages. This compares with 708,000 divorces in 1970, an increase of nearly 64%!

Today it is much worse than 1910. The latest figures we could find, early in the 21st century, showed 2,355,005 marriages and 957,200 divorces.

In Dallas some time back, one 3-lawyer firm boasted of handling up to 3,000 divorces a year, which averages out at about 4 divorces per work day for each attorney. One of the lawyers in the firm convinced Family Court Judge Linda Thomas to perform divorces for 54 couples at once. The 108 individuals raised their right hands in unison and Judge Thomas declared them all divorced. The time involved was barely 11 seconds per person. That is about the same time as the Arabic Bedouin, who needs only to say to his wife 4 times, "I divorce thee!" What a farce this is to the sanctity and sacredness of marriage.

Unfortunately, Christians are also succumbing to this sin in increasing numbers. Some say the statistics show little difference between saved and lost – and some figures actually claim the "redeemed" are out-divorcing the "pagans."

Not only so, but fashion trends in our nation exalt suggestiveness and nudity. Hemlines are up and necklines are down. One would have to look twice at some women on many bathing beaches to ascertain they were not stark naked – and on some beaches they are! The sex pervert can get a bigger thrill visiting a supermarket at mid-afternoon than he formerly could by attending a nudist convention. Women of our day appear publicly in a state of undress that a harlot would have been embarrassed about a generation or so ago.

Movies, theaters, local show productions, night clubs, and numerous other mediums of entertainment emphasize lewdness and suggestiveness. Filth is found on our newsstands by the ton, available to either young or old with money enough to make the purchase. Unfortunately, the verses of Proverbs 6:27-28 are still true: "Can a man take fire in his bosom, and his clothes not be burned? Can one go upon hot coals, and his feet not be burned?" No one can play with sex fire and not suffer the searing torture of permanent pain.

What should we say about prostitution, pornography, R- and X-rated movies, the homosexual/lesbian uprising, rape, incest, the AIDS epidemic and all the rest? If we don't have revival, if we don't get back to the "old paths," this country is gone. Not only so, it is getting to where America *deserves* to suffer the fate of Babylon, Rome and other great empires before her.

She needs also to repair the old-fashioned standards of honesty and integrity. Today's philosophy of "the world owes me a living" has the curse of God upon it. Everyone wants something for nothing. For the most part, people at the polls vote for the politician who makes the most promises and offers the most attractive socialist program. The "pork barrels" in politics are there only because people back home are greedy and have larceny in their bones.

This same philosophy has caused the gambling compulsion to become a major American problem. According to Michael MacDougall, a leading gambling detective in Washington, D.C., "Gambling is the biggest business in America today – bigger than steel, the movies or the auto industry." To take advantage of this human weakness, almost every State in the Union has entered the gambling business with some form of lotteries for raising revenues. Magazine subscriptions are sold, not because people like to read but because they think they might win a $10,000,000 jackpot! With horse racing, dog racing, bingo, poker, the numbers racket, and 101 other forms of legal and illegal gambling, the total tab comes to around $177 billion annually. *U.S. News & World Report* was right in calling it "an epidemic."

Even worse, the Federal Bureau of Investigation reported crime figures for one year showing nearly 13,211,000 recorded cases of murder, robbery, forcible rape, aggravated assault, larceny, auto theft and burglary – more than 25 every minute around the clock, day and night. This was up more than 65% above what it was 25 years earlier, right here in so-called "Christian" America!

Child abuse and neglect cases that year totaled 1,299,400, more than double what it was only 7 years previously. Even with these astounding statistics, the number one crime problem of our day is not included: the flood of illegal narcotics of every form that is destroying this country and stealing the brains of its citizens. (By way of example, there were 300,000 more arrests for drug abuse violations than DUI charges!) In this country, there were 5.6 murders for every 100,000 citizens in 2002. Excluding burglaries, Philadelphia (City of Brotherly Love!) led all crime levels that same year, above the national average in murder, forcible rape, robbery, aggravated assaults, larceny/theft and motor vehicle theft. Incidentally, according to the Bureau of Justice Statistics, in one recent year among the 5.3 million convicted offenders under the jurisdiction of our corrections agencies, almost 2 million were estimated to have been drinking when they committed their crime.

Our annual crime bill is in the billions! The last records available to me showed approximately 680,000 Americans locked up behind bars in our jails and penitentiaries. That is one person incarcerated for every 365 citizens in the land – men, women, children *and babies!* How we need to repair the old-fashioned standards of honesty and integrity in this country! Altogether, in 2004 there were 14,004,327 people arrested for breaking laws in this country.

For years, we have been told that education is the answer. In the last year for which the government has supplied figures, a total of 979,477,000 bachelor's degrees, 286,251,000 master's degrees, 32,943,000 doctor's degrees and 614,749,000 post-secondary degrees below a bachelor's, such as associate degrees, were granted. Yet smarter has not been better, unless you count making criminals more sophisticated. Some of the most profitable illegal activity in our day has been through "insider trading" among the elite of Wall Street. And it is beginning to look as if we will need more jails just to handle the CEOs and politicians being shipping off to prisons.

Furthermore, the standards of sobriety and temperance need to be repaired in this nation. In one of my "Incidents & Illustration" columns, I reported census bureau figures showing, at that time, we had 192,000 bartenders and only 167,000 ministers of the gospel; one tavern for each 326 people, old and young; and 213,955 more liquor bars in this country than churches. There is no evidence that the sordid record is any better today.

Since the repeal of the 18th Amendment – one of America's sorriest acts – we have spent literally billions on booze. The result is that the United States is fast becoming a nation of drunks – the polite, politically correct word is "alcoholics" – who are excused as being victims of a "disease" (which would be a joke if not so tragic). Depending on what figures you use, there are probably at least 20 million of those "diseased folks" in our country today. According to Tim Campbell, the economic cost to society from alcoholism and alcohol abuse are estimated at nearly $117 billion a year, including $18 billion from premature deaths, $66 billion in reduced work effort, and $13 billion for treatments.

Some of the worst abusers are our national leaders. Harry Ferguson, a United Press International reporter, referring to drinking in our nation's capital, once said, "Any person with governmental, diplomatic or journalistic connections who is not suffering from a communicable disease can easily attend 1,450 cocktail parties a year, or about 4 a day. These are not small gatherings in living rooms, but alcoholic mass meetings with a receiving line and an orchestra." *God help America!*

America now produces or imports 156 million gallons of distilled spirits per year, 773.3 million gallons of wine, 201.2 million barrels (31 gallons per barrel) of beer. That is enough for every person 18 years of age or older in the country to consume 4.63 gallons of distilled spirits, 5.29 gallons of wine, and 64.3 gallons of beer annually! The State of Ohio, which has for its official State motto, "With God All Things Are Possible," through its Department of Liquor Control, is reportedly "the world's largest buyer of spirits."

Booze is the big killer on our highways. In 2004, on weekends, 51% of all fatal crashes were alcohol-related and even during the week, 30% of those fatalities had the same cause. Alcohol is also responsible for approximately 40% of all crimes (both violent and non-violent) committed annually in this country. Figures show that the average alcohol-related fatality in the United States costs $3.5 million ($1.1 million in monetary costs; $2.4 million in quality of life losses). It is hardly worth it, is it?

Unfortunately, this liquor problem is not just a concern among the unconverted. Many of the current popular and respected Bible teachers are decrying what they call "legalism," insisting that a little nip is all right for today's church members. Such encouragement for social drinking is all that most worldly, carnal Christians need, and social drinking is becoming more and more acceptable even in evangelical churches. Many of their members now drink wine with meals and have beer (which the Bible calls "strong drink") in the refrigerator. Some are even sampling the really hard stuff without any qualms of conscience. We have liberated ourselves right into powerlessness and ineffectiveness in our service to God and man.

The *Holman Standard Bible*, since distillery was unknown in Bible times, has rightfully translated the phrase "wine and strong drink" throughout Scripture as "wine and beer." See, for example, where Isaiah 5:11 is correctly and accurately translated, "Woe to those who rise early in the morning in pursuit of beer, who linger into the evening inflamed by wine." And statisticians tell us beer "is the drink of choice in most cases of heavy drinking, binge drinking, drunk driving and underage drinking."

B. In Our Worship Centers

This Old Gate also needs to be repaired in our churches. For one thing, there is a desperate need to get back to an old-fashioned reverence for God, His day and His Name. It is an unusual Christian who truly gives over to God the Lord's Day in the 21st century. It has become – even among God's people – a day of pleasure, joy riding, picnics, yard work, ball games, swimming, visiting relatives, and everything imaginable under the sun. It is no longer in reality a holy day, but a holiday coming once every week, with an occasional 4-day weekend thrown in for good measure!

The children of our generation are not being taught that Sunday is a day of worship, praise and thanksgiving to God, but that it is a day of special outside activities – with church only playing a small part, *if at all*. Hundreds of thousands of children in America look forward to Sunday, yes, not because it means attending Sunday school, but rather to find out what happened to some cartoon character after he was struck with 100,000 volts of electricity in last week's TV episode on the Sunday cartoons.

Our churches also need to repair the old-fashioned prayer meeting. Many have done away with the prayer meeting completely and churches still having it seem to consider them meetings for women and children. Even thriving evangelical churches have made the prayer meeting into another preaching service with prayer only an incidental factor. However, the church that gives up its prayer meeting had better give up! Prayer is the backbone, the foundational pillar of a New Testament church.

Our churches also need to repair the preaching of the old-fashioned gospel of Christ. Pulpits across the country are filled with so-called moderates (formerly called liberals or modernists) who deny the verbal, inerrant inspiration of the Scripture, the blood atonement, our Lord's virgin birth, His bodily resurrection, the miracles, salvation by grace through faith, Heaven, Hell, and just about everything else the Word of God teaches.

Some time ago a prison chaplain friend of mine handed me a book, *The Living Bible* (not the paraphrase by that name released by Tyndale Publishing House). Edited by a Bolton Hall, a publishers' blurb on the cover said: "A great deal of the Bible consists of sheer repetition and scores of duplications. By elimination and condensation of matter which has never played an appreciable part in the ordinary reader's sense of the Bible and its value, this book presents the entire content of the Old and New Testaments in a third of the bulk to which ten generations of English readers are accustomed."

In other words, Mr. Hall threw out two-thirds of the Bible as incidental, if not worthless. The insinuation is that the Holy Spirit did not know what He was doing when He included the other two-thirds. Fortunately for both the world and God, the idea seems to be, Bolton Hall eliminated the divine error and produced a superior Bible. That is the height – or rather, *depth* – of subtle blasphemy!

What is Hall's Bible like? By way of example, checking I & II Chronicles, I discovered that these 65 chapters had been condensed into less than two pages! Turning to this 3rd chapter of Nehemiah, I found that, according to Hall's *Living Bible*, there would be no series of messages entitled "Gateways to Glory." Mr. Hall entirely eliminated the entire portion as unimportant, a section merely cluttering up and encumbering the Word of God.

However, II Timothy 3:16-17 still say: "All scripture is given by inspiration of God, and is profitable for doctrine, for reproof, for correction, for instruction in righteousness: that the man of God may be perfect, throughly furnished unto all good works."

"All Scripture" is God-breathed! As such, it is *all* profitable, not merely one-third of it. (Incidentally, Bolton Hall did not have the courage to insert these words of Paul to Timothy in his 'bulkless' Bible. Possibly he didn't dare!)

Since Mr. Hall's fiasco, the Reader's Digest Corporation, through its Condensed Book Projects division, released an abbreviated Bible, using the RSV text, which eliminated about 40 percent of the Old Testament and 25 percent of the New Testament, calling the omitted portion "repetition, rhetoric and redundancy!" *What unmitigated gall!*

My point is this: isn't it indicative of a need to repair the Old Gate in America's churches when such blasphemy can be introduced without vehement protest on the part of scarcely anyone? How we need a brand new generation of John the Baptists, Jeremiahs and Pauls, to say nothing of Spurgeons, Torreys, Truetts, Moodys, Luthers and Wesleys!

I want you to note, however, that the Fish Gate comes *before* the Old Gate. The new convert is to immediately use his zeal in trying to bring others to Christ, not wait until he has been trained in theological soundness. Philip, in his witness to Nathanael, is an illustration of this fact. John 1:45 tells us, "Philip findeth Nathanael, and saith unto him, We have found him, of whom Moses in the law, and the prophets, did write, Jesus of Nazareth, **the son of Joseph**" (emphasis added). Philip had not yet learned the truth about Messiah's supernatural conception by the Holy Spirit in the womb of the virgin, yet he rightly set out to bring Nathanael to Jesus – *and he did!*

Let me briefly insert the timely reminder that this Old Gate needs repairing in our churches by the return of the old-fashioned method of financing God's work. His plan is not through sales, suppers, bazaars, car washes, magazine subscriptions, raffles, Bingo parties, or kindred insults to the holiness of God, but through tithes and offerings. Believe it or not, Americans give less than $3 billion yearly to all religious causes – *compared with more than $10 billion for booze!* Year after year sees "Christian America" giving as much as four times for booze alone – not counting other financial waste – as its inhabitants do for God.

God's plan of financing His work is in tithes and offerings. And, thank God, that system still works for all who follow it. He promised, *"Bring ye all the tithes into the storehouse, that there may be meat in mine house, and prove me now herewith, saith the Lord of hosts, if I will not open you the windows of heaven, and pour you out a blessing, that there shall not be room enough to receive it"* (Malachi 3:10).

C. In Our Homes

This Old Gate also needs repair in our homes. For one thing, we need to repair the old-fashioned family altar. Statisticians tell us that 90 percent of our church members *never* have family worship in their homes. When we get away from this custom we have lost the most sacred thing in family life. My father was not converted until I was almost in my teens and we *sometimes* had a family altar after that, but mother wrote me years later that it was her life's greatest regret that we did not have family worship in our home on a *regular* basis.

May I suggest to you that a home without a family altar, with no grace before meals, with no exalting of God's Word, is not worshiping and honoring God as it should? Might I also charge that although there are Christians in the home, the home itself is not Christian?

When ex-President Grover Cleveland faced death at Princeton, his thoughts were not on past political battles or presidential honors; instead, his mind slipped back over the years to his boyhood days in the Presbyterian manse. Daily his godly father had gathered the family around him for reading the Sacred Scriptures and followed with earnest prayer. Small wonder that this man who had received America's highest honors called for an old hymnal, through which he met death with its message in music!

This leads me to another matter, the return of old-fashioned music in our homes. We have long enough exalted, in Christian homes, the music *written* by the devil's crowd, *published* by the devil's crowd, *recorded* by the devil's crowd, *sold* by the devil's crowd, *bought* by the devil's crowd, *sung* by the devil's crowd, *danced to* by the devil's crowd, and *praised* by the devil's crowd. Keep in mind that even a secular, scientific periodical like the *Medical Review* has claimed that dance music *alone* arouses sexual appetites.

It is wrong to use God's property to sing Satan's songs! Our voices, our tongues, our lips are God's – bought with a price – and are to be used for His glory alone. Away with rock 'n' roll, country, western, and all other forms of music which exalt the world, the flesh and the devil. It does not belong in the home of a child of God. We are not saying that all such forms of music are wrong, but merely the kind exalting the world, the flesh and Satan.

In thinking about repairing the Old Gate in our homes, note that in our text Jedaiah was repairing "over against his house" (Vs. 10), and with the ruler of the half part of Jerusalem, Shallum, it was also a family repair job. Verse 12 tells us "he and his daughters" were working together, something which must have been thrilling to behold, as father and daughters united in serving Jehovah God.

One more question needs answering before we leave this gate in Christian experience, namely,

III. THE PROGRAM: *How Does this Old Gate Need to be Repaired?*

A. *In Our Proclamation*

We need to stick to the old paths *in our profession*, in our words. This relates to what we believe and what we teach. It calls for preaching that honors the historic fundamentals of the faith once delivered. It necessitates crying out boldly and uncompromisingly against sin and calling for repentance. The prophets of old thundered out against the evils of their day, and God-blessed preachers down through the centuries have done the same! Yet how rare in our time are men with courage to do so! They are, truly, America's vanishing breed. In fact, many of our so-called super churches are open in frankly admitting they do not mention anything negative, boasting instead that they are "seeker friendly."

It also calls for preaching which holds up the cross and reveals the simplicity of salvation. It is tragically true that one could attend thousands of churches across America for months – including some sound, orthodox ones – and never hear how to be saved.

Do you remember Paul's holy vow? He shared it with the Corinthians, telling them, "For I determined not to know any thing among you, save Jesus Christ, and him crucified" (I Corinthians 2:2). He simply meant that all of his preaching would center around the cross. True, he preached the whole counsel of God, as he reminded the Ephesian elders (Acts 20:27), but he made certain that the road in his message, at some point, went by the cross.

Is this true in *your* church?

In Our Practice

Again, this Old Gate needs to be repaired by sticking to the old paths *in what we do and how we live!* This relates to our daily living. To do so requires *yielded* living. As Romans 12:1-2, express it: "I beseech you therefore, brethren, by the mercies of God, that ye present your bodies a living sacrifice, holy, acceptable unto God, which is your reasonable service. And be not conformed to this world: but be ye transformed by the renewing of your mind, that ye may prove what is that good, and acceptable, and perfect, will of God."

It also calls for *separated* living. The solemn insistence for the people of God is in II Corinthians 6:17, "Wherefore come out from among them, and be ye separate, saith the Lord, and touch not the unclean thing; and I will receive you." This idea has been completely lost in some of our churches.

But yielded living and separated living are no more necessities than *dependent* living. By this I mean what Jesus meant when He told His disciples in John 15:5, "... without me ye can do nothing." All of our service must be entirely and utterly reliant upon Him. This dependency is to be manifested daily in the believer's life, especially through prayer and Bible study.

In Our Program

We need to repair this Old Gate not only by sticking to the old paths in our profession and in our practice, but also *in our agenda*. The church program of the 1st century is the only really workable one for the 21st century. In Acts 5:42, that program of the early Christians is succinctly summed up: "And daily in the temple, and in every house, they ceased not to teach and preach Jesus Christ." How does this compare with the program at your church today?

Oh, let's leave the paths of despair and darkness and get back to the paths of hope and light, the pathways where true rest is found. God help our country, our churches and our homes to rebuild this Old Gate. We have the promise in II Chronicles 7:14, "If my people, which are called by my name, shall humble themselves, and pray, and seek my face, and turn from their wicked ways; then will I hear from heaven, and will forgive their sin, and will heal their land."

We are told by some that times have changed, that we are too old-fashioned, and that we need to bring our religion up-to-date.

Why?

Other things haven't changed. Sin, sorrow, death, eternity, Heaven, Hell and kindred truths are still the same. God is the same. He has promised, "For I am the LORD, I change not ..." (Malachi 3:6). The Word of God says of our Savior, "Jesus Christ the same, yesterday, and to day, and for ever" (Hebrews 13:8).

Salvation is the same. Acts 10:43 assures us, "To him give all the prophets witness, that through his name whosoever believeth in him shall receive remission of sins." And, by the same token, "Neither is there salvation in any other: for there is none other name under heaven given among men, whereby we must be saved" (Acts 4:12). As has been true for thousands of years, simply "believe on the Lord Jesus Christ, and thou shalt be saved, and thy house" (Acts 16:31).

Herbert Buffum has summed up our sentiments precisely, writing,

> Well, they say it is better,
> "Things have changed, don't you know,"
> And the people in gen'ral
> seem to think it is so;
> And they call me old-fashioned
> when I dare to say,
> That I like it far better
> in the old-fashioned way.
>
> If the Lord never changes,
> as the fashions of men,
> If He's always the same,
> why He is old-fashioned then!
> As an old-fashioned sinner
> saved thro' old-time grace,

Oh, I'm sure He will take me
to an old-fashioned place.

'Twas an old-fashioned meeting,
in an old-fashioned place,
Where some old-fashioned people
had some old-fashioned grace;
As an old-fashioned sinner
I began to pray,
And God heard me, and saved me,
in the old-fashioned way.

Thank God for the Old Gate!
Let's restore it in our lives and rebuild it in our churches.

Chapter 5

THE VALLEY GATE!

"The valley gate repaired Hanun, and the inhabitants of Zanoah; they built it, and sat up the doors thereof, the locks thereof, and the bars thereof, and a thousand cubits on the wall unto the dung gate."

– Nehemiah 3:13

Which gate is this in Christian experience? Perhaps some, in thinking of valley, might automatically suggest Psalm 23:4, "Yea, though I walk through the valley of the shadow of death, I will fear no evil: for thou art with me; thy rod and thy staff they comfort me," but this could not possibly be. The gates are in progressive order and this is only the fourth with six to go. It is too early for the undertaker, for the Christian to be taking off for Heaven.

The application is found in the word "valley" itself. The dictionary defines it as "a low point or interval in any process, representation, or situation." Ordinarily we think of it as a low tract of land situated between mountains or hills. All of us have experienced a time when, driving in unfamiliar country, we topped a hill and had our breath sucked in as we suddenly beheld the striking beauty of some deep valley beneath us.

Which direction is the valley? It is down, of course, and that is the point for us. A valley is something very low. This gate speaks of something almost totally forgotten in this egocentric age in which we live, where everyone seems concerned with having the right "self-esteem" and looking out for "Number One." It speaks of humility. This is truly a lost virtue today and it seems as absent from the life of our average professing Christian as it does from the lost sinner who has dedicated his life to getting ahead of the Joneses, not merely keeping up with them.

James 4:10 pinpoints the Lord's command for His own: "Humble yourselves in the sight of the Lord... ." For us, it is not a *suggestion*;

it is *an order* from the lips of our Commander-in-Chief. In thinking of this virtue it might be well to remember what another has noted, namely, "Humility is not thinking less of yourself; it is thinking of yourself less."

The two names associated with this gate offer additional confirmation that humility is indeed the correct application. For example, the only worker mentioned individually is Hanun, which means "gracious," certainly one of the fruits of a humble walk before the Lord. And the name of the city where the rest of the workers originated, Zonoah, has an even stronger relationship to humility, since it means "broken."

If this is the true application of the Valley Gate – and we are convinced it is – how desperately it calls for repairing and rebuilding in our churches and among all of our church people today. It is urgently needed in pulpit and pew alike. A common prayer, especially among Southerners, is, "Lord, keep me humble!" Yet that petition is itself an evidence of pride because the individual is implying he is *already* humble and is only asking the Lord to help him remain that way. Preachers sometimes joke, "Have you read my latest book, *Humility: And How I Got That Way?*"

We even use pride as a figure of speech, something considered good. For example, someone may say, "I am proud to meet you," or, "I am proud to be here tonight." We talk about being proud of our family, proud of our church, proud of our house, proud of our car, and proud of a thousand-and-one other things. Pride is seen as something good, not something bad; something to be desired, not something to be shunned.

Years ago I read a story about a young minister, fresh out of the seminary, who had been sent by his bishop to his first parish at a remote country church. When he rose to the pulpit that first Sunday morning and looked out over his poorly dressed and seemingly illiterate congregation, he thought to himself, "Oh, my, how awful that I must bury my vast talents and education in this situation for any length of time." Obviously, he was not being overwhelmed with a spirit of humility.

Unbeknown to him, however, after that first service and sermon, one of the church stewards got alone and cried to God, "Dear Lord, take this inexperienced and unprofitable young man and develop him sufficiently to where he will be capable of remaining as the permanent pastor of our flock."

We cannot help but wonder if this story does not illustrate every one of us? Probably only the circumstances and the details are different. Our pride, nine times out of ten, is based on something without any ground in reality. While valid in all walks of life, it is especially true in the spiritual realm. The person most obsessed with how spiritual he or she is, usually is the one who knows the least and who really possesses the least spirituality.

Pride has always been a serious problem. The other day we were reading a book written some 200 years ago by an old Scottish Presbyterian preacher. George Lawson, discussing Genesis 43:19, noted: "Joseph's brethren could not, in their younger days, bear the thought of bowing down before him, yet now they court the favor of Joseph's servants. Beware of pride. You know not by what changes in the affairs of this changeable world your loftiness may be bowed down. Some have been compelled by hard necessity to bow down before those whom they would once have disdained to set with the dogs of their flocks. That haughty spirit which sets itself in opposition to the will of God goes before a fall." Indeed, *it does!*

Benjamin Franklin was not even a professing Christian, but he warned, "In reality there is perhaps no one of our natural passions so hard to subdue as pride. Disguise it, struggle with it, beat it down, stifle it, mortify it as much as one pleases, it is still alive, and will now and then peek out and show itself."

The dear Lord knows that there is pride in all of us. While the noted poet William Cowper was speaking of sin in general, his words are aptly suited to this sin of pride:

> It twines itself about my thoughts,
> And slides into my prayer.

And so it does. James 4:3 is an illustration: "Ye ask, and receive not, because ye ask amiss, that ye may consume it upon your lusts."

Even those who claim to be humble are proud of it. Dear friends, this ought not so to be! God expects us – yea, *commands* us – to be humble. He warns us of the consequences of not being humble, noting the deadly danger in pride. He forbids new converts taking pastoral leadership for this very reason, saying in I Timothy 3:6, "Not a novice, lest being lifted up with pride he fall into the condemnation of the devil." And pride, of course, is listed as one of the things God hates (Proverbs 6:17; 8:13).

If one needs an illustration of what pride can do, it is only necessary to look at what it did to Satan. He was one time, perhaps, the most important person in Heaven under the Trinity. What caused him to fall to his present position as the number one archenemy of God? The story is recorded in Isaiah 14:12-15:

> *"How art thou fallen from heaven, O Lucifer, son of the morning! how art thou cut down to the ground, which didst weaken the nations! For thou hast said in thine heart, I will ascend into heaven, I will exalt my throne above the stars of God: I will sit also upon the mount of the congregation, in the sides of the north: I will ascend above the heights of the clouds; I will be like the most High. Yet thou shalt be brought down to hell, to the sides of the pit."*

Note the root of his problem, saying in his heart, "**I** will …, **I** will …, **I** will …, **I** will …, **I** will," five times. The same element of pride is seen again in Ezekiel 28:12-18, where we read:

> *"Thus saith the Lord God; Thou sealest up the sum, full of wisdom, and perfect in beauty. Thou hast been in Eden the garden of God; every precious stone was thy covering, the sardius, topaz, and the diamond, the beryl, the onyx, and the jasper, the sapphire, the emerald, and the carbuncle, and gold: the workmanship of thy tabrets and of thy pipes was prepared in thee in the day that thou wast created. Thou art the anointed cherub that covereth; and I have set thee so: thou wast upon the holy mountain of God: thou hast walked up and down in the midst of the stones of fire. Thou wast perfect in thy ways from the day that thou wast created, till iniquity was found in thee. By the multitude of thy merchandise they have filled the midst of thee with violence, and thou hast sinned; therefore I will cast thee as profane out of the mountain of God; and I will destroy thee, O*

covering cherub, from the midst of the stones of fire. Thine heart was lifted up because of thy beauty, thou hast corrupted thy wisdom by reason of thy brightness: I will cast thee to the ground, I will lay thee before kings, that they may behold thee. Thou hast defiled thy sanctuaries by the multitude of thine iniquities, by the iniquity of thy traffick; therefore will I bring forth a fire from the midst of thee, it shall devour thee, and I will bring thee to ashes upon the earth in the sight of all them that behold thee."

What happened? His heart was lifted up because of his beauty. *Pride!*

Not only was pride the original sin in all eternity, it was also the first sin of mankind. The full story is told in the opening chapters of the Word of God, but note especially the words of Satan to Eve about the forbidden fruit, and her response in Genesis 3:5-6: *"God doth know that in the day ye eat thereof, then your eyes shall be opened, and ye shall be as gods, knowing good and evil. And when the woman saw that the tree was good for food, and that it was pleasant to the eyes, and a tree to be desired to make one wise, she took of the fruit thereof, and did eat, and gave also unto her husband with her; and he did eat."*

It should be clear from these examples what tragic fruit results from pride – Satan lost his heavenly paradise while Adam and Eve lost their earthly paradise – and why God warns His people so strongly against it from Genesis to Revelation, urging them to walk in paths of humility. Even the emblems of Scripture highlight this truth.

Since this gate speaks of humility, it is significant that after Nehemiah had taken his initial tour of the ruined holy city, it says about his trip back to his camp, "Then went I up in the night by the brook, and viewed the wall, and turned back, and entered by the gate of the valley, and so returned" (2:15). That he was humbled by what he had seen is indicated by his use of the Valley Gate to return to his quarters.

Years ago, from a now unknown source, we clipped the following:
"Of all the mighty, stately trees, God chose the lowly plant that creeps along a helpful wall, the vine, with which to illustrate. Of all the beasts, God chose the soft and patient lamb. Of all the fowls God chose the mild and guileless dove. Christ is the

rose of the field, and the lily of the valley. When God appeared unto Moses, it was not in the lofty cedar, nor the sturdy oak, nor the stately elm, but in a bush; a humble, slender, shrub; actually a thorn bush, the lowliest of all trees. Every language of the Scriptures portrays an attempt by God to check the conceited arrogance of man."

Let's look at some of that language.

I. THE TEMPTATION: *Don't Overestimate Yourself!*

"For I say, through the grace given unto me, to every man that is among you, not to think of himself more highly than he ought to think: but to think soberly, according as God hath dealt to every man the measure of faith" (Romans 12:3).

This chapter starts, after 11 doctrinal chapters, the practical side of Paul's epistle to the saints at Rome, most of whom he had never met. It begins with a plea for absolute consecration to God on the part of every Christian (Vss. 1-2) and the first thing the apostle notes after that dedication of the life to Him is humility (Vs. 3). Evidently the Holy Spirit of God, who put into the heart and mind of Paul what to pen and where to write it, places a very high evaluation upon this lowly attitude.

Notice that Paul says he speaks "through the grace given unto" him. That is, on the basis of his apostolic authority and apostolic wisdom. And he addresses his remarks to "every man" among them. What is that plea to each and every Christian? "Not to think of himself more highly than he ought to think."

It is suggestive to note that he did not warn his readers not to think highly of themselves, but "more highly than [they] ought." You see, we *are* to think highly in some respects. We should think highly of ourselves in the sense that we are too good to be the slaves of sin, Satan and the world. We should think highly of ourselves in the sense that we are the children of God, His ambassadors to this world. We should think highly of ourselves in the sense that we are dressed in the robes of Christ's own righteousness. We should think highly of ourselves in the fact that we are owners of a heavenly inheritance, including a clear title to a mansion in the Glory Land. But in each of these instances the reason for thinking highly is based totally upon what Christ has done *for* us and offers no ground for personal fleshly pride.

How are we to think of ourselves? Paul says "soberly"; that is, we are to have a sober opinion of self. In ourselves we have nothing of which to be proud. It would be well to remember what some satirist once said, "The cemeteries are filled with people who thought the world wouldn't be able to get along without them." The best of us are only poor, wretched, miserable sinners saved by His marvelous, fathomless grace. We are compelled to say with Paul, "I know that in me (that is, in my flesh,) dwelleth no good thing" (Romans 7:18).

Take heed that you do not think too highly of yourself.

Do not think too highly of *your abilities*. As I Corinthians 4:7 points out: "For who maketh thee to differ from another? and what hast thou that thou didst not receive? now if thou didst receive it, why dost thou glory, as if thou hadst not received it?"

Do not think too highly of *your performances*. There is a danger, both as individuals and as churches, to think great results are the consequence of *our* actions and so we boast of our deeds and accept the credit that belongs to Him and Him alone. We are not against numbers – God has a whole book by that name in the Pentateuch – but we *are* against anyone stealing glory which belongs to God.

Do not think too highly of *your judgments*. This is where our stubbornness comes in: we have too high an opinion of our opinions! We have a tendency to think we are always right about everything, from a wide range that covers the finest points of theology to the kind of breakfast food that is the most nourishing and beneficial for a day's right start.

The lesson all of us need to learn is recorded in Jeremiah 9:23-24: "Thus saith the LORD, Let not the wise man glory in his wisdom, neither let the mighty man glory in his might, let not the rich man glory in his riches: but let him that glorieth glory in this, that he understandeth and knoweth me, that I am the LORD which exercise lovingkindness, judgment, and righteousness, in the earth: for in these things I delight, saith the LORD." Or, as Paul put it: "No flesh should glory in his presence ... according as it is written, He that glorieth, let him glory in the Lord" (I Corinthians 1:29, 31).

Consider next,

II. THE TECHNIQUE: *The Quickest Way Up is Down!*

"*At the same time came the disciples unto Jesus, saying, Who is the greatest in the kingdom of heaven? And Jesus called a little child unto him, and set him in the midst of them, and said, Verily I say unto you, Except ye be converted, and become as little children, ye shall not enter into the kingdom of heaven. Whosoever therefore shall humble himself as this little child, the same is greatest in the kingdom of heaven. And whoso shall receive one such little child in my name receiveth me*" (Matthew 18:1-5).

The disciples were attempting here to put an earthly value on heavenly things. They were thinking of honor, position, prestige, acclaim, supremacy, glory – the things men and women sell their souls for in this life attempting to gain.

Our Lord pointed out that the humblest in this sphere of activity will be the most exalted in His Kingdom. He said, "Whosoever therefore shall humble himself as this little child, the same is greatest in the kingdom of heaven."

Here is incentive for even the least gifted, the least educated, the least talented among us. It harmonizes perfectly with what Paul wrote in I Corinthians 1:26-29: "*For ye see your calling, brethren, how that not many wise men after the flesh, not many mighty, not many noble, are called: but God hath chosen the foolish things of the world to confound the wise; and God hath chosen the weak things of the world to confound the things which are mighty; and base things of the world, and things which are despised, hath God chose, yea, and things which are not, to bring to naught things that are; that no flesh should glory in his presence.*"

The now defunct *Sunday School Times* once quoted Charles Fox on "God's five-ranked army decreasing human weakness." Regarding this army, any can enlist if they are:

Foolish enough to depend on Him for wisdom;
Weak enough to be empowered with His strength;
Base enough to have no honor but God's honor;
Despised enough to be kept in the dust at His feet;
Nothing enough for God to be everything.

Years ago a Baptist magazine called attention to a fascinating fact that probably never once entered the mind of most of us: "Have you ever thought of it, that only the smaller birds sing? You never heard a note from the eagle in all your life, nor from the turkey, nor from the ostrich. But you have heard from the canary, the wren, and the lark. The sweetest music comes from those Christians who are small in their own estimation and before the Lord."

As the old spiritual expresses it,

> The quickest way up is down,
>   The quickest way up is down;
> You may try and try to climb up high,
>   But the quickest way up is down.

Consider next,

III. THE TEST: *"Big Shot"* or *"Servant"*?

Matthew 20:20-28 tells a fascinating story:

> *Then came to him the mother of Zebedee's children with her sons, worshipping him, and desiring a certain thing of him.*
>
> *And he said unto her, What wilt thou? She saith unto him, Grant that these my two sons may sit, the one on thy right hand, and the other on the left, in thy kingdom.*
>
> *But Jesus answered and said, Ye know not what ye ask. Are ye able to drink of the cup that I shall drink of, and to be baptized with the baptism that I am baptized with? They say unto him, We are able.*
>
> *And he saith unto them, Ye shall drink indeed of my cup, and be baptized with the baptism that I am baptized with: but to sit on my right hand, and on my left, is not mine to give, but it shall be given to them for whom it is prepared of my Father.*
>
> *And when the ten heard it, they were moved with indignation against the two brethren.*
>
> *But Jesus called them unto him, and said, Ye know that the princes of the Gentiles exercise dominion over them, and they that are great exercise authority upon them.*
>
> *But it shall not be so among you: but whosoever will be great among you, let him be your minister;*

And whosoever will be chief among you, let him be your servant:
Even as the Son of man came not to be ministered unto, but
to minister, and to give his life a ransom for many.

Once again, as so often with our Lord's disciples and with us today, fleshly ambition had risen to the top. In Mark's account, he tells us that James and John joined their mother in making the request – it was not hers alone. At any rate, it resulted in Jesus giving another discourse on humility. The Son of God pointed out that "the princes of the Gentiles exercise authority" (Vs. 25), but warned, "It shall not be so among you" (Vs. 26).

Contrary to the world's view, Jesus explained, herein lies the *true* test of greatness: **humility!** And this humility finds its expression, He emphasized, in service to others; *in ministering!* In short, the man or woman who is truly great is the one who is always eager to minister to others.

If you would like a reverse illustration of what not to be and do, consider III John 9-11:

I wrote unto the church: but Diotrephes, who loveth to have
the preeminence among them, receiveth us not.
Wherefore, if I come, I will remember his deeds which he
doeth, prating against us with malicious words: and not content
therewith, neither doth he himself receive the brethren, and for-
biddeth them that would, and casteth them out of the church.
Beloved, follow not that which is evil, but that which is
good. He that doeth good is of God: but he that doeth evil hath
not seen God.

In words unmistakable, John tells us that seeking the preeminence in the church "is evil," not "good."

A. The Example of Our Savior, the Son of God

Here is how Paul expressed it:

Let this mind be in you, which was also in Christ Jesus:
Who, being in the form of God, thought it not robbery to be
equal with God:

> *But made himself of no reputation, and took upon him the*
> *form of a servant, and was made in the likeness of men:*
> *And being found in fashion as a man, he humbled himself,*
> *and became obedient unto death, even the death of the cross.*

As the poet put it, "Oh, to be like Him!"

One illustration of how He totally humbled Himself can be seen in John 13, where the eternal, omnipotent God of the universe is seen on His knees, washing and drying the dirty feet of His disciples. And the example was followed by the instruction: *"Ye call me Master and Lord: and ye say well; for so I am. If I then, your Lord and Master, have washed your feet; ye also ought to wash one another's feet. For I have given you an example, that ye should do as I have done to you. Verily, verily, I say unto you, The servant is not greater than his lord; neither he that is sent greater than he that sent him. If ye know these things, happy are ye if ye do them"* (Vss. 13-17).

If one example is worth a thousand words, this speaks several volumes!

IV. THE TIP: *Don't Grab a Box Seat!*

Using the illustration of a wedding, we are told that Christ:

> *... put forth a parable to those which were bidden, when he*
> *marked how they chose out the chief rooms; saying unto them,*
> *When thou art bidden of any man to a wedding, sit not down*
> *in the highest room; lest a more honourable man than thou be*
> *bidden of him;*
> *And he that bade thee and him come and say to thee, Give this*
> *man place; and thou begin with shame to take the lowest room.*
> *But when thou art bidden, go and sit down in the lowest*
> *room; that when he that bade thee cometh, he may say unto thee,*
> *Friend, go up higher: then shalt thou have worship in the pres-*
> *ence of them that sit at meat with thee.*
> *For whosoever exalteth himself shall be abased; and he that*
> *humbleth himself shall be exalted* (Luke 14:7-11).

In the land and day of the Lord, guests were seated at banquets and given guest rooms according to their position and stature in the community. The most important received the best, and the least the poorest – just as is common today, when the Senator is seated at the President's table and the director of the Humane Society is at a table near the kitchen door.

Jesus warned His disciples to start out taking the least and then being honored, perhaps, with an invitation to move up. The person who takes one of the best positions at the beginning stands a chance of being humiliated when the host or hostess asks him to move down. Pride can, indeed, prove very embarrassing.

But we are not just talking about what can happen at the hands of our fellow men. The Lord Himself will humble us if we don't do so ourselves. Consider some of these scriptural statements:

"Every one that is proud in heart is an abomination to the LORD: though hand join in hand, he shall not be unpunished ... Pride goeth before destruction, and an haughty spirit before a fall" (Proverbs 16:5, 18).

"A man's pride shall bring him low ..." (Proverbs 29:23).

"I will punish the world for their evil, and the wicked for their iniquity; and I will cause the arrogancy of the proud to cease, and will lay low the haughtiness of the terrible" (Isaiah 13:11).

"Likewise, ye younger, submit yourselves unto the elder. Yea, all of you be subject one to another, and be clothed with humility: for God resisteth the proud ..." (I Peter 5:5).

The latter verse offers a two-fold choice that faces every Christian: (1) humbling himself and receiving grace; or, (2) feeling the resisting, chastening hand of God upon his life.

One of the most dynamic illustrations of what can happen to the proud is seen in the life of perhaps the greatest, most powerful world ruler of all time, Nebuchadnezzar, the king of Babylon. He was lifted up with pride, you will recall, and ended up eating grass with the oxen. While the full story is told in Daniel 4, the divinely inspired author summarized it in the next chapter when interpreting the handwriting on the wall for his grandson, King Belshazzar:

> *O thou king, the most high God gave Nebuchadnezzar thy*
> *father a kingdom, and majesty, and glory, and honour:*
> *And for the majesty that he gave him, all people, nations,*

*and languages, trembled and feared before him: whom he would
he slew; and whom he would he kept alive; and whom he would
he set up; and whom he would he put down.*

*But when his heart was lifted up, and his mind hardened in
pride, he was deposed from his kingly throne, and they took his
glory from him:*

*And he was driven from the sons of men; and his heart was
made like the beasts, and his dwelling was with the wild asses:
they fed him with grass like oxen, and his body was wet with the
dew of heaven; till he knew that the most high God ruled in the
kingdom of men, and that he appointeth over it whomsoever he **will*** (5:18-21, emphasis added).

King Saul is another illustration of ruin from pride. When he was
little in his own sight, he was "made the head of the tribes of Israel,
and the LORD anointed thee king over Israel" (I Samuel 15:17), but
when he was lifted up with a sense of his own importance, he lost the
kingdom and was tragically humbled before his own people.

The pitiful stories of the world's Nebuchadnezzars and Sauls are
written in the archives of time. Let them be a warning and a lesson to
us all.

Now let's get to the heart of rebuilding the Valley Gate.

V. THE TREATMENT: *How to Humble Yourself!*

*"Draw nigh to God, and he will draw nigh to you. Cleanse your
hands, ye sinners; and purify your hearts, ye double minded. Be
afflicted, and mourn, and weep: let your laughter be turned to mourning, and your joy to heaviness. Humble yourselves in the sight of the
Lord, and he shall lift you up"* (James 4:8-10).

Obviously, the closer we get to the majestic God of the Bible, the
lower we will become in our own estimation – and in actual reality.
One surely could not remain long in the presence of the Holy One of
Israel – Jehovah-Tsidkenu, "the Lord our Righteousness" – and be
consumed with a feeling of personal importance. The secret to humility, then, is drawing nigh to God.

The fact that the closer we draw to Him the more insignificant and
lowly we will consider ourselves is illustrated in the life of Job.

Throughout the book, as he defends himself against the charges of his friends, his feelings of self-righteousness become more and more apparent. Yet look at the conclusion, where he confesses to God, "I have heard of thee by the hearing of the ear: but now mine eye seeth thee. Wherefore **I abhor myself**, and repent in dust and ashes" (Job 42:5-6, emphasis added). When he saw the Lord he abhorred himself.

But how does one "draw nigh to God"? The answer is, of course, *through Bible study and prayer!* He talks to us as we read His Word; we talk to Him when we pray. It is that simple (or, perhaps, that difficult).

What will happen when we draw nigh to Him? "He shall lift you up."

A. Before Men!

He will lift us up *in the sight of man*. Isn't that the essence of what we saw in Matthew 20? Our Lord promised, "...whosoever will be great among you, let him be your minister; and whosoever will be chief among you, let him be your servant."

B. In Ministry!

He will lift us up *in successful service*. It is as a prolific, fruitful fisherman explained his secret: "First, keep yourself out of sight. Second, keep yourself further out of sight. Third, keep yourself still further out of sight."

In Christian service, this is what the old-timers called "hiding behind the cross." Remember the Lord's promise in Isaiah 66:2, "...to this man will I look, even to him that is poor and of a contrite spirit, and trembleth at my word."

C. In Closeness to Him!

He will lift us up *in close communion and fellowship with Himself*. As we have seen, while one with a proud, haughty spirit cannot come very close to Jehovah God, the reverse is true for the individual with a humble and contrite spirit. Yes, indeed, the quickest way up is down.

Conclusion

Be honest, dear reader, is this Valley Gate torn down and burned with fire in your Christian life? Does it need repairing? You cannot make any advances in your Christian experience until it is repaired.

Action, not talk, is needed here. We heard of one brother who prayed, "Lord, make me a doormat," but when another trod upon him a short time later his reaction was anything but an example of humility. Or love. Or victory.

Here is a divine challenge: "Humble yourselves therefore under the mighty hand of God, that he may exalt you in due time" (I Peter 5:6). Not only is this a challenge about humility, it is a promise of exaltation as He sees fit, according to His perfect time schedule.

This is also how revival comes: "If my people, which are called by my name, **shall humble themselves**, and pray, and seek my face, and turn from their wicked ways; then will I hear from heaven, and will forgive their sin, and will heal their land" (II Chronicles 7:14, emphasis added).

As an evangelist with over a half-century in the harvest, I can assure you that the very first step in the revival process is, "shall humble themselves." There are no shortcuts, no end runs around it, no quick fixes.

May God help us all to rebuild our Valley Gates!

Chapter 6

THE DUNG GATE

"But the dung gate repaired Malchiah the son of Rechab, the ruler of part of Bethhaccerem; he built it, and set up the doors thereof, the locks thereof, and the bars thereof."

– Nehemiah 3:14

Webster's Approved Dictionary defines dung as "anything filthy or rotten." This was the gate through which all the rubbish, the defilement, the garbage and the waste of the city was removed. Just outside the Dung Gate was the Valley of Gehenna, which served as the city dump and was where all the debris from the city was burned. Here the fire burned continuously and was the location our Savior used as an illustration of Hell.

In fact, the Dung Gate was also called the Rubbish Gate. It stands in Christian experience for a clean, consistent life – with all the world's defilement removed. The hinges on this gate need to be well oiled for frequent use and it goes without saying that unless such is true, there will be no real peace, blessing or fruit for the believer in His service.

Actually, however, the Dung Gate stands for removal of more than mere defilement. Paul spoke of his own personal righteousness and the things whereof he "might trust in the flesh," and then said, "But what things were gain to me, those I counted loss for Christ. Yea, doubtless, and I count all things but loss for the excellency of the knowledge of Christ Jesus my Lord: for whom I have suffered the loss of all things, **and do count them but dung**, that I may win Christ" (Philippians 3:7-8, emphasis added).

If we learned our lesson well at the Valley Gate, we should have no trouble at this one. But if *that* lesson was not learned, we can expect all kinds of problems here at the Dung Gate, since it is only as we humble ourselves in the sight of the Lord that we have the capability to fully see the filth and rubbish clogging up our lives – and the grace to remove it.

Job is an outstanding example of this truth and it was not until he humbled himself that he realized how truly abominable his self-righteousness was in the sight of a holy God. His testimony to Jehovah at that time was: "I have heard of thee by the hearing of the ear: but now mine eyes seeth thee. Wherefore I abhor myself, and repent in dust and ashes" (Job 42:5-6).

This is a gate all need to use frequently, not just the so-called backslider. I do not mean that we need repeated cleansing for our souls in salvation, but that our hearts, our minds, our lives need frequent washing. This truth was illustrated by Christ before the Feast of the Passover when, after having dined with His disciples, He arose, laid aside His outer garments, took a towel, girded Himself, poured water into a basin, and began to wash His disciple's dirty feet, wiping them with the towel fastened around His waist. When it came Peter's turn, he protested, insisting, "Thou shalt never wash my feet."

When the Lord replied, "If I wash thee not, thou hast no part with me," Peter cried, "Lord, not my feet only, but also my hands and my head."

We can understand how Peter felt, but that was when Jesus said: "He that is washed needeth not save to wash his feet, but is clean every whit: and ye are clean, but not all. For he knew who should betray him; therefore said he, Ye are not all clean" (John 13:10-11).

Here was an object lesson which taught vital spiritual truth the disciples did not understand at the time. Obviously, this was more than a mere foot washing since Jesus said, "What I do thou knowest not now" (Vs. 7).

Here was a beautiful picture of those who had experienced a once-for-all salvation bath, making the disciples clean "every whit." (Since Judas was not saved, he was not clean in *any* sense, as verse 11 notes.) Yet the bathed disciples still got dirty feet in their daily pilgrimage and their journey to the upper room proved it; their feet were dirty. They did not need another bath, another salvation cleansing, but they *did* need to have their feet washed. So it is today; those who have been converted do not need to get saved all over again when they sin, but they do need a daily foot washing *from* and *through* and *by* the Word of God.

I repeat, all need to use the Dung Gate frequently since none has attained to perfect holiness. Our situation is like the one in Nehemiah's day, when it was testified, "there is much rubbish" (4:10) and the Jews were "not able to build the wall" (4:10) because of it.

While it is true that some in our day claim to have reached perfection, their lives do not back up the assertion. Paul pointed out in Galatians 5:16-17 that all of us have fleshly weaknesses. He was compelled to write: "This I say, then, Walk in the Spirit, and ye shall not fulfill the lust of the flesh: and these are contrary the one to the other: so that ye cannot do the things that ye would."

The Apostle John noted the same imperfection in all when he wrote: "If we say that we have no sin, we deceive ourselves, and the truth is not in us ... If we say that we have not sinned, we make him a liar, and his word is not in us" (I John 1:8, 10).

Let us learn some lessons from the Dung Gate phase of our Christian experience.

I. THE PROBLEM: *Why Cleanse Our Lives?*

The simplest and obvious answer is: *they need it!*

It is true that some need cleansing to a lesser degree and some to a larger one, but *all* need it.

Second, we need to cleanse our lives because God has *commanded* us to do so. It is in I Thessalonians 4:7 that we read, "For God hath not called us unto uncleanness, but unto holiness." Then Peter strongly urged, "But as he which hath called you is holy, so be ye holy in all manner of conversation; Because it is written, Be ye holy: for I am holy" (I Peter 1:15-16).

The sin of uncleanness is contrary to the very nature and design of our calling in Christ. Just as the Old Testament law forbade impurity, offering any number of ceremonial cleansings to prove it, so the gospel calls its followers from uncleanness to holiness.

After one of the strongest passages found anywhere in the Word of God relative to separated living, the 7th chapter of II Corinthians opens with the words: "Having therefore these promises, dearly beloved, let us cleanse ourselves from all filthiness of the flesh and spirit, perfecting holiness in the fear of God." Note that we are to cleanse ourselves from "*all* filthiness." There is to be no partial cleansing, no half-way business. Oh, that every Christian would get busy, might really figuratively roll up the sleeves and start shoveling the filth from his or her life.

Third, we should cleanse our lives because of what will be true in the life if it is not cleansed. Failure here will hurt every phase of the Christian's personal life. It doesn't take much wrong to do tremendous damage. Our Lord's human brother, when talking about one specific form of uncleanness, exclaimed in James 3:5, "Behold, how great a matter a little fire kindleth!"

Any physician can tell you that bad tonsils will send poison throughout the whole body, affecting the entire physical system. Any dentist will tell you that bad teeth sometimes affect the complete body and nervous system in a similar manner. This is true of other fleshly weaknesses and, in like manner, sin in any part of our life will throw out its poison and affect all of our life.

Again, one cannot be an effective soul winner if his life is not clean. At the Dung Gate, only one man, Malchiah, is mentioned in the rebuilding. We are told that he was a ruler of part of Beth-haccerem, which means, "the place of the vineyard." Here is a reminder of the truth that believers are branches of Christ, the Vine, and He expects us to bear much fruit. Vineyards must be kept clean in order to be productive. The unproductive vineyard in Isaiah 5 was laid waste, not pruned nor digged, and choked with briars and thorns. In Christ's reference to His vineyard in John 15, He speaks of the purging necessary to produce "fruit," "more fruit," and "much fruit."

The wise man, Solomon, told of observing how uncleanness has an effect on productivity. He wrote: "*I went by the field of the slothful, and the vineyard of the man void of understanding; And, lo, it was all grown over with thorns, and nettles had covered the face thereof, and the stone wall thereof was broken down. Then I saw, and considered it well: I looked upon it, and received instruction. Yet a little sleep, a little slumber, a little folding of the hands to sleep: So shall thy poverty come as one that travelleth; and thy want as an armed man*" (Proverbs 24:30-34).

Hence, those who want to be effective in service for Jehovah are told: "Depart ye, depart ye, go ye out from thence, touch no unclean thing; go ye out of the midst of her; be ye clean, that bear the vessels of the Lord" (Isaiah 52:11). What a vital matter personal holiness is in His service!

Furthermore, if the life is not clean, the servant will quickly become a stumbling block to others. Often people have asked me, "Will I be lost if I do thus and so?" If you have really received Jesus Christ as your personal Savior and have been born again, it is possible for you to do things that will not send you to Hell, *but they may send someone else to Hell!* Romans 14:7 warns, "For none of us liveth to himself, and no man dieth to himself."

Everyone has influence, some conscious and some unconscious – but all of it very real. Years ago I read of a clock in the window of a jewelry store which stopped one morning for thirty minutes exactly at 8:15. Folks who were hurrying to work slowed down and had a leisurely visit with one another. School children running to their classes, stopped and played along the way. Professional men, seeing the time on the face of the clock, stopped and chatted one with another.

The result was that all were late to work, school and business just because one little clock had stopped running for 30 minutes. It made them aware of how unconsciously they had been depending upon the jeweler's clock. You, too, may not know how others are depending upon your testimony – and they may not realize it, either – but that does not change the fact that they are and that if your life is unclean it will cause others to stumble. Perhaps they will fall and not be able to rise.

On the other hand, if your life is kept consistently clean, you can really draw nigh to God and He will draw nigh to you. Surely all are aware of the truth that it is impossible to draw nigh to God with filthy, unclean lives.

All prayer will be ineffectual and powerless if the life is unclean. The psalmist was aware of this and testified, "If I regard iniquity in my heart, the Lord will not hear me" (Psalm 66:18). And Isaiah declared: "Behold, the Lord's hand is not shortened, that it cannot save; nor his ear heavy, that it cannot hear: But your iniquities have separated between you and your God, and your sins have hid his face from you, that he will not hear" (Isaiah 59:1-2).

Oh, that your prayer and mine might ever be: "Who can understand his errors? cleanse thou me from secret faults. Keep back thy servant also from presumptuous sins; let them not have dominion over me: then shall I be upright, and I shall be innocent from the great transgression" (Psalm 19:12-13).

II. THE PARTICULARS: *Of What Shall We Cleanse Our Lives?*

We learn the answer to this in the verse mentioned a moment ago, II Corinthians 7:1: "Having therefore these promises, dearly beloved, let us cleanse ourselves from all filthiness of the flesh and spirit, perfecting holiness in the fear of God."

We must cleanse our lives of all "filthiness of the flesh;" that is, *the sins of the body*. Adultery, lasciviousness, idolatry, fornication, drunkenness, gluttony, reveling and such like are not to be found. Our present generation has tried to dress up and glamorize these vices, but they are the same old dirty, rotten sins history has always known.

Again, we are to cleanse our lives of all "filthiness of the ... spirit"; that is, *the sins of the heart, the mind, and the soul*. These involve such sins as lying, pride, vanity, deceit, wicked imaginations, temper, vain rattlings of the tongue, divisions, hate, lack of faith, arrogance, doubt, gossip, unbelief, and sins of such temperament.

If you are in doubt if something is sin or not, here is the simple test to determine whether it is or not. First Corinthians 10:31 says, "Whether therefore ye eat, or drink, or whatsoever ye do, do all to the glory of God." And Colossians 3:17 tells us, "And whatsoever ye do in word or deed, do all in the name of the Lord Jesus, giving thanks to God and the Father by him."

Can you *eat* it, or *drink* it, or *do* it to the glory of God? Can you do it in His Name, giving thanks to the Father for it? If you cannot do so honestly, then it is sin! Remember, too, that sin is sin in God's sight and the subtle terminology of our day which catalogs sin into *little* and *big* is a philosophy not found within the covers of the Holy Bible.

We are to "cleanse ourselves from all filthiness of the flesh and spirit"; and we are to "perfect holiness in the fear of God!"

III. THE PLAN: *How Shall We Cleanse Our Lives?*

First of all, consider it from the negative standpoint. This cleansing will not be brought about in our own strength. The scriptural promise does not say, "**I** can do all things."

How many have tried to gain cleansing through the arm of the flesh and hopelessly failed! In fact, on numerous occasions Christians have told me they have honestly, truly, earnestly tried to get victory over some particular matter – and absolutely could not do it.

I do not believe them! Either they lied, or God lied when He promised that victory was available and attainable.

All failure in cleansing can be summed up in two principal reasons: (1) The sinning Christian has not fully trusted Christ to help him; or, (2) he really does not want to be cleansed; he loves the sin too dearly. But victory is available for all those who really want it and for those who will trust Christ for it.

This brings us to the positive consideration of cleansing. First, the secret is in prayer. The battle will have to be fought on your knees. The more time spent in supplication to God, the more grace and strength you will receive from Him, hence the easier it will be.

Second, the cleansing will come through the Word of God. In that marvelous 119th Psalm, we are told in verse 9 how to *gain* the victory: "Wherewithal shall a young man cleanse his way? by taking heed thereto according to thy word." Then in verse 11 we are told how to *keep* the victory: "Thy word have I hid in mine heart, that I might not sin against thee."

The Apostle Paul, in mixing his teaching about church and marriage relationships, wrote: "Husbands, love your wives, even as Christ also loved the church, and gave himself for it; That he might sanctify and cleanse it with the washing of water by the word, That he might present it to himself a glorious church, not having spot, or wrinkle, or any such thing; but that it should be holy and without blemish" (Ephesians 5:25-27).

There are many other clear statements revealing to the children of God that daily cleansing comes through His Word. In John 15:3, Jesus told His disciples: "Now ye are clean through the word which I have spoken unto you." And in His high priestly prayer, He pleaded with the Father about His followers, "Sanctify them through thy truth: thy word is truth" (John 17:17).

However, not only should this cleansing be sought prayerfully and through the Scriptures, but it must be sought *honestly*. The issue is not whether we think some matter is right or wrong, but does it really glorify God? I fear there are many things we do not weigh honestly simply because we do not want to know the truth about them. We know what will happen if we learn it. Yet a believer will not know real effectiveness in his life until he honestly evaluates that life in the holy, heavenly scales of biblical righteousness.

Finally, this cleansing must be sought *thoroughly*. I mean by this, the ridding from our lives of *every* sin God points out to us through His Holy Spirit. Our cleansing should be akin to that of a careful housewife who never ceases her scrubbing as long as a speck remains on floor or furniture. Or perhaps a better illustration would be the scrubbing of a surgeon before going into the operating room; failure for cleaning here might result in the infection and death of another. We must not be satisfied as long as any known sin is in the life. Do not allow any refuse to pile up on the Dung Gate of your Christian experience.

IV. THE PERIOD: *When Should We Cleanse Our Lives?*

Begin *now!*

This is a gradual process. While a *soul* can be and is cleansed immediately and eternally the moment one trusts Christ as Lord and Savior, no *life* can be completely cleansed instantaneously. Rome wasn't built in a day and no young believer becomes a mature Christian overnight. Instead, it is a matter of "*perfecting* holiness," as we saw in II Corin-thians 7:1.

The thought is for aggressive action. It is the "*growing* in grace and knowledge" of II Peter 3:18. Sanctification works the same as does going to the bad. No one becomes a hardened sinner overnight. And neither does one become a mature saint apart from a gradual growth.

However, as you humble yourself before God and submit to Him, He will point out, one by one, what things in your life should go. The important thing is *to start!*

It is vital also to realize that this cleansing must be repeated regularly, sometimes daily. Occasionally even hourly! Old sins creep back in and new ones crop up. The Christian life, of necessity, is one of self-purifying through the means of grace made available by our Lord and Savior, Jesus Christ.

I recall my father telling of an experience from his boyhood. It seemed that he and his brothers had a cat their mother determined must be "put away." The lads decided that the most humane (!) manner for its 'execution' would be death by drowning (an electric chair or lethal injection was not available to them), so they proceeded to make all the arrangements. Getting a burlap bag, they placed the cat securely inside, tying the end with a rope and weighting it down with a huge stone.

They then took their improvised "casket" to the Chenango River, which flowed through the eastern outskirts of their town. Walking out on the bridge that crossed the river, they dropped their weighted sack in the middle, into the deepest part. Sadly they watched the air bubbles rise from the rippling water and then, reluctantly, trudged homeward.

Playing along the way, as boys are wont to do, they eventually arrived home late that afternoon. Imagine their surprise – tempered by childish joy, of course – when they walked to the rear of the house and saw the cat sunning himself on the back porch, trying to dry his wet fur!

When I told that story in Northern Ohio one time, a lady came up to me after the service and said, "Brother Sumner, that bag must have had a hole in it some where!"

So it did! And the bags in which we seek to drown our sins seem to have holes in them, too, so it is a battle that must be fought repeatedly.

Dear Christian, if you really love Jesus Christ, will you, by the grace of God, resolve that your remaining years will be of real *service* – inspired by real *consecration?* How it behooves us to live consistently, without being a stumbling block to others. To quote the words of Jehovah God again: "Depart ye, depart ye, go ye out from thence, touch no unclean thing; go ye out of the midst of her; *be ye clean, that bear the vessels of the Lord*" (Isaiah 52:11, emphasis added).

Chapter 7

THE FOUNTAIN GATE!

"But the gate of the fountain repaired Shallun the son of Colhozeh, the ruler of part of Mizpah; he built it, and covered it, and set up the doors thereof, the locks thereof, and the bars thereof, and the wall of the pool of Siloah by the king's garden, and unto the stairs that go down from the city of David.

"After him repaired Nehemiah the son of Azbuk, the ruler of the half part of Bethzur, unto the place over against the sepulchres of David, and to the pool that was made, and unto the house of the mighty.

"After him repaired the Levites, Rehum the son of Bani. Next unto him repaired Hashabiah, the ruler of the half part of Keilah, in his part.

"After him repaired their brethren, Bavai the son of Henadad, the ruler of the half part of Keilah.

"And next to him repaired Ezer the son of Jeshua, the ruler of Mizpah, another piece over against the going up to the armoury at the turning of the wall.

"After him Baruch the son of Zabbai earnestly repaired the other piece, from the turning of the wall unto the door of the house of Eliashib the high priest.

"After him repaired Meremoth the son of Urijah the son of Koz another piece, from the door of the house of Eliashib even to the end of the house of Eliashib.

"And after him repaired the priests, the men of the plain.

"After him repaired Benjamin and Hashub over against their house. After him repaired Azariah the son of Maaseiah the son of Ananiah by his house.

"After him repaired Binnui the son of Henadad another piece, from the house of Azariah unto the turning of the wall, even unto the corner.

"Palal the son of Uzai, over against the turning of the wall, and the tower which lieth out from the king's high house, that was by the court of the prison. After him Pedaiah the son of Parosh."

– Nehemiah 3:15-25

This gate speaks of the Spirit-filled life, a vital part of every fruitful child of God. Springs in Scripture repeatedly refer to life overflowing with and through the Holy Spirit of Almighty God. They are symbols of freshness, of beauty, of life, and of dynamic power.

For example, in John 4:14, Jesus said to the Samaritan woman at the well of Sychar, *"Whosoever drinketh of the water that I shall give him shall never thirst; but the water that I shall give him shall be in him a well of water springing up into everlasting life."* There are two kinds of wells: one is a simple reservoir where accumulated water is stored; the other contains the waters of a spring. Obviously, the latter is referred to here because Jesus described it as "springing up."

In the seventh chapter of John, Jesus again used the same kind of language about thirsting, drinking and water springing up to flow. On this occasion, at the feast of tabernacles, we read: *"In the last day, that great day of the feast, Jesus stood and cried, saying, If any man thirst, let him come unto me, and drink. He that believeth on me, as the scripture hath said, out of his belly shall flow rivers of living water"* (Vss. 37-38).

In the very next verse this symbolic language is explained in a parenthetical passage, using language impossible to misunderstand: "But this spake he of the Spirit, which they that believe on him should receive: for the Holy Ghost was not yet given; because that Jesus was not yet glorified."

It is not, therefore, fantasy or speculation to say that the application of this gate can be summed up in the words of Ephesians 5:18: "And be not drunk with wine, wherein is excess; **but be filled with the Spirit**" (emphasis added).

Let me remind you again of the definite, distinct, progressive order found in these gates. The lessons must have been learned at the previous gates before the Gate of the Fountain can be fully experienced. This is especially true of the lessons of the last two gates, the Valley Gate and the Dung Gate. A fountain cannot flow when choked by stones and rubbish, nor can the blessed Holy Spirit fill that which is already preoccupied with self and cluttered with sin and its fruits.

Mentioned in an earlier chapter was Nehemiah's returning by the Valley Gate after his first tour of the city. It is noteworthy in the spiritual lessons of these gates that at that time, "Then I went on to the gate of the fountain, and to the king's pool: but there was no place for the beast that was under me to pass." In short, he wanted to return through the Gate of the Fountain, but he could not. No one can benefit from this Gate until he has been to the Valley Gate and then the Dung Gate to clean up his life.

We think it significant also that the only man named in repairing the Dung Gate was Malchiah, who ruled part of Beth-haccerem. The name of that city means "House of the Vineyard." One wanting the blessing of the sweet fruit in God's vineyard will be anxious to repair the Dung Gate in his life!

This gate dealing with the fullness of the Holy Spirit is one especially needed by Christian leaders. We previously emphasized that Rephaiah and Shallum, the co-leaders of Jerusalem, were associated with the Old Gate. In preparing this message, our thoughts turned to the fact that here was surely a gate where the experience and blessing of spiritual leaders was desperately needed. Wondering if rulers were mentioned here, we turned to the passage to inquire.

Here is what we discovered: Shallun, the ruler of part of Mizpah, worked directly on this gate (Vs. 15). Nehemiah, the ruler of the half part of Beth-zur, worked in this section (Vs. 16); as did Hashabiah, the ruler of the half part of Keilah (Vs. 17); Bavai, the ruler of the other half part of Keilah (Vs. 18); and Ezer, the ruler of Mizpah (Vs. 19). In other words, *rulers are mentioned at the Gate of the Fountain two and one-half times more than at any other gate in the wall!*

It is also highly significant that, at this gate representing the Spirit-filled life, was "the house of the mighty" (Vs. 16). How strong and powerful in Christian service is the ministry of a Spirit-filled believer!

Since many Christians do not understand what the Spirit-filled life is all about, let's ask and scripturally answer some questions about it. First of all,

I. THE BACKGROUND: *What is Necessary for a Spirit-Filled Life?*

A. Regeneration

The first requirement is a salvation experience. Until an individual has experienced the new birth – what theologians call regeneration –

he or she cannot expect to live a Spirit-filled life.

Before going farther it might be well to explain that the *indwelling* of the Holy Spirit and the *infilling* of the Holy Spirit are two separate, distinct duties of the Spirit of God. Some erroneously understand Ephesians 5:18 to mean, "Let the Holy Spirit of God come into your life!" *Such is definitely not the case!*

According to the Word of God, the Holy Spirit indwells *all* believers. Every individual who has been born again has the Holy Spirit dwelling within him. First Corinthians 6:19-20 presents this truth as something startling and unusual for any Christian *not* to realize: *"What? know ye not that your body is the temple of the Holy Ghost, which is in you, which ye have of God, and ye are not your own? For ye are bought with a price: therefore glorify God in your body, and in your spirit, which are God's."*

In Ephesians 1:13 we are told: "In whom ye also trusted, after that ye heard the word of truth, the gospel of your salvation; in whom also after that ye believed, ye were sealed with that holy Spirit of promise." Here we are assured that the moment we believed the Word of Truth, the Gospel, we were "sealed" with the Holy Spirit.

Actually, for an individual not to have the Holy Spirit dwelling in his body is definite proof that he or she is lost and on the road to eternal damnation. Romans 8:9 puts it bluntly: "Now if any man have not the Spirit of Christ, he is none of his." Note that "Spirit of God" and "Spirit of Christ" are used interchangeably and both refer to the blessed Holy Spirit, a Person of the Trinity. For one not to have God's Spirit means that he is "none of His," hence lost and Hell-bound.

The same truth is borne out in Galatians 4:6 when we are told, "And because ye are sons, God hath sent forth the Spirit of his Son into your hearts, crying, Abba, Father." God's Holy Spirit dwells in our heart and teaches us to cry out in supplication, "Father, our Father."

My elemental theology professor in seminary, who also taught me two years of systematic theology, Dean Emory H. Bancroft, talking about the infilling of the Holy Spirit, correctly said: "It may occur at conversion, and is to be sought afresh in each new emergency or act of service." And so it should.

B. A Knowledge of the Word of God

But there is more to the Spirit-filled life than merely experiencing salvation. It is also necessary to have a knowledge of the Word of God. God does not fill scriptural ignoramuses with His Holy Spirit. *It takes a Scripture-filled Christian to be a Spirit-filled Christian!*

Since the power of a hydrogen bomb is like a child's Fourth of July sparkler in comparison to the power of the Holy Spirit, it is only logical that God insists we know how to use His power before He entrusts us with it.

C. A Hunger for His Fullness

Third, an earnest desire for the Spirit-filled life is necessary. It is significant to note that in verse 20 of our text it speaks of Baruch "earnestly" repairing his section. And note also that this earnest working was at the "door of the house" of the high priest!

An earnest desire for the Spirit-fullness has been a prerequisite for His special ministry in every dispensation. In the Old Testament, God's people were told, "For I will pour water upon him that is thirsty, and floods upon the dry ground: I will pour my Spirit upon thy seed and my blessing upon thine offspring" (Isaiah 44:3). Thirsting was essential to Jehovah's pouring of water and flooding arid ground, which He Himself expressly described as the pouring out of His Spirit upon them.

We find the same teaching in the New Testament. When the disciples of Jesus besought Him to teach them to pray as John the Baptist had taught His disciples, our Lord gave them what is known as the Lord's Prayer. Following it, He gave them a lesson about importunity in prayer, reciting the story of the empty-cupboard friend who knocked on his neighbor's door at midnight, begging bread for a third party who had suddenly arrived at his home in the middle of the night.

Jesus climaxed the lesson with this application: "If a son shall ask bread of any of you that is a father, will he give him a stone? or if he ask a fish, will he for a fish give him a serpent? or if he shall ask an egg, will he offer him a scorpion? If ye then, being evil know how to give good gifts unto your children: *how much more shall your heavenly*

Father give the Holy Spirit to them that ask him?" (Luke 11:11-13, emphasis added). Here in language clear and simple, Jesus taught His disciples to earnestly desire the fullness of the Holy Spirit and to ask for that very thing!

Some object that Jesus told His disciples this *before* the Holy Spirit had come to dwell within believers and, therefore, it is wrong now to pray for the Holy Spirit. But they are confusing the matter of indwelling and infilling. All believers are indwelt by the Holy Spirit, but not all believers are filled with the Holy Spirit, as indicated by the command of Ephesians 5:18. It is unnecessary to pray for the Holy Spirit to come and dwell in a believer's body, of course, but it is right and proper to pray for – *and earnestly desire* – the fullness of the Spirit in the life.

Actually, the suggestion that it is wrong to pray for the Holy Spirit, an error unfortunately helped along by a footnote in the Scofield Reference Bible, is a "Johnny-come-lately" idea. Old-time theologians, Bible teachers and anointed evangelists never dreamed of such a distinction. They all took it for granted that Jesus meant what He said and that Christians of every age should pray for the Holy Spirit's fullness in their lives. You can search in vain in the writings of saints of old for a suggestion that praying for the Holy Spirit is improper. Not a word will be found.

John R. Rice, so greatly used as an evangelist in the 1900s, in answering Scofield in this, wrote: "I would be gentle here. I would not willingly cause a moment of grief to any Christian brother who differs with me. And yet I feel that some good men have robbed God's people of their heritage, have unwittingly aided apostasy, have unwittingly hindered revival by teaching people that they are not to pray for that which Jesus encouraged us to pray ... Oh, may God give us a revival, and conviction and souls saved, and the blessing and power of God upon His people, at whatever cost! Oh, how dearly some of us may pay if we discourage God's people from seeking the power of the Holy Ghost to do the will of God!"

Saintly Matthew Henry wrote: "Observe, (1) the direction he gives us what to pray for. We must ask for the Holy Spirit, not only as necessary in order to our praying well, but as inclusive of all the good things we are to pray for ... Note, The gift of the Holy Ghost is a gift we are every one of us concerned earnestly and constantly to pray for."

And one of the finest of the older commentaries, *The Pulpit Commentary* , commenting on Luke 11:13, says: "Here the Lord ... pictures the case of one who deserves a special deepening of the spiritual life, and prays some prayer for the presence of the Holy Spirit. Such a prayer, says Christ, must be granted." And again, the same commentary says: "We have only, in conclusion, to emphasize the fact that the Holy Spirit is the great need of human souls. Let us ask Him as God's supreme Gift and we shall assuredly receive Him even in Pentecostal power. It is this Gift which individuals and churches need to make them truly useful."

Let me quote again my systematic theology professor, Dean Emery H. Bancroft, who expressed it like this: "The Scriptures make mention of only one baptism of the Holy Spirit, while the infilling of the Spirit is not confined to a single experience, but may be repeated times without number. There need be no long searching before receiving this. It may occur at conversion, *and is to be sought afresh in each new emergency or act of service"* (emphasis added).

While there are numerous other authorities we could quote, this is sufficient to establish the point. However, we do not need to rely on human commentaries to definitely and conclusively prove that it is right and proper – even since the coming of the Holy Spirit to indwell the believer – to pray for His fullness. In Acts 4:31, at a time in church history when no one will deny that the Holy Spirit was already indwelling believers, we read: "And when they had prayed, the place was shaken where they were assembled together; and they were all filled with the Holy Ghost, and they spake the word of God with boldness." Note the positive statement: *"when they had prayed, ... they were filled with the Holy Ghost."* Here the disciples were "filled with the Holy Ghost" in response to definite, believing prayer.

Incidentally, these nine words, "and they were all filled with the Holy Ghost," are the same identical nine words used in describing the Pentecostal experience of Acts 2:4. At that time, also, the fullness of the Holy Spirit came after earnest, believing prayer – in that case, after 10 days of such intercession at the Throne.

D. Humility and Cleanliness

In addition to salvation, a knowledge of the Word, and an earnest desire to be filled, two other prerequisites for a Spirit-filled life are humility and cleanliness. We will not deal with them here because the two previous messages have considered them in detail. Suffice it to say now that victories at the Valley Gate and the Dung Gate are imperative for victory at the Gate of the Fountain.

E. Prayer

A final prerequisite we will mention is prayer. As our Lord expressed it: "If a son shall ask bread of any of you that is a father, will he give him a stone? or if he ask a fish, will he for a fish give him a serpent? Or if he shall ask an egg, will he offer him a scorpion? If ye then, being evil, know how to give good gifts unto your children: **how much more shall your heavenly Father give the Holy Spirit to them that ask him?**" (Luke 11:11-13, emphasis added).

By way of example, that prince of pulpiteers, Charles Haddon Spurgeon, in his sermon on Acts 10:44, "The Outpouring of the Holy Spirit," said: "And, best of all, if you would have the Holy Spirit, let us meet together to earnestly pray for Him. Remember, the Holy Spirit will not come to us as a church unless we seek Him."

America's greatest evangelist, Dwight Lyman Moody, in referring to the passage in Luke 11:13, said, "Now the lesson to be learned from this is, that we must pray for the Holy Spirit for service; pray that we might be anointed and qualified to do the work that God has for us to do … We have to ask for this blessing, to knock for it, to seek for it, and find out why it does not come."

II. THE BRANDS: *What Are the Evidences of a Spirit-Filled Life?*

All kinds of confusion, heresy and misunderstanding centers around this question. Because of this fact, it will be well first to consider matters that are *not* confirmation of His fullness.

A. Things That Are NOT Evidence

The Holy Spirit's gifts, described in I Corinthians 12, are not evidence of the fullness of the Spirit in a believer's life. In verse 11 of that chapter, immediately after listing the gifts, we read, "But all these worketh that one and the selfsame Spirit, dividing to every man severally as he will."

Note the words "to every man." Evidently all Christians have some gift although it may never be used and, in some cases, perhaps never even discovered. Paul urged young Timothy to "stir up the gift of God, which is in thee" (II Timothy 1:6). Likewise, while Ephesians 4:8 tells us that the ascended Christ "led captivity captive, and gave gifts unto men" – and Psalm 68:18, from which Paul quoted in his Ephesian letter, added, "yea, for the rebellious also" – still Ephesians 5:18, with its command to be filled, makes it clear that not all are controlled by this member of the Trinity.

This is borne out clearly in studying the Corinthian church. In the opening of his first letter to them, Paul said: "I thank my God always on your behalf ... that ye come behind in no gift" (Vss. 4, 7), yet he opened the third chapter by saying, "And, I, brethren, could not speak unto you as unto spiritual, but as unto carnal, even as unto babes in Christ." The Christians at Corinth all had some gift or gifts – as a matter of fact, many theologians feel they were the most gifted church in the New Testament era – yet they were not "spiritual," which is another way of saying they were not Spirit-filled. They were carnal, and the real value of their gifts was never realized in the lives and service of most of them.

Another matter often mistakenly considered as evidence of the Holy Spirit's fullness is speaking with tongues. While this frightfully abused, horribly misused, totally misunderstood subject by some groups is not within the scope of this message, please remember that the word "tongues" always means "*languages*," nothing more.

While we do not have space to present a study of scriptural tongues here, suffice it to simply say that it could *not* be a sign of the Holy Spirit's fullness since the Word of God teaches it is a sign for lost people, not for the saved. We are told in I Corinthians 14:22, "*Wherefore tongues are for a sign, not to them that believe, but to them that believe not: but prophesying serveth not for them that believe not, but for them which believe.*"

Neither is speaking with power an evidence, in itself, of the Holy Spirit's fullness. Some base this idea on the fact that Jesus told His disciples, just before returning to Heaven, "But ye shall receive power, after that the Holy Ghost is come upon you: and ye shall be witnesses unto me both in Jerusalem, and in all Judaea, and in Samaria, and unto the uttermost part of the earth." Yet there is clear evidence that this power was not in speaking, but in boldness, courage and kindred virtues of faithful witnessing.

Some of the greatest orators in America today, able to sway great crowds, are clearly not Spirit-filled men, not humbly walking with God. They can wax eloquent, give a open invitation, and the altars will be filled – yet the majority of the "converts" are nowhere to be found six months later. Alas, sometimes in six weeks!

The Apostle Paul was obviously a man mightily filled with God's Spirit, yet he reminded the Corinthians that their description of him was, "his bodily presence is weak, and his speech contemptible" (II Corinthians 11:10). If speaking with power were the evidence of a Spirit-filled life, there would be no need for our non-leaders to be filled, yet it is a command for the least among us.

B. Things That ARE Evidence

What, then, is the evidence? Actually, it is three-fold.

First, there is the *evidence which others can see*, the fruit of the Spirit manifested in the life. Galatians 5:22-23 say: "But the fruit of the Spirit is love, joy, peace, longsuffering, gentleness, goodness, faith, meekness, temperance: against such there is no law."

It is more important that others know you are filled than for you to know it yourself. If you are scripturally filled with God's Spirit, you will not have to tell anyone; they will know it.

Someone has used the fruit tree as a case in point to illustrate this evidence. The fruit tree belongs to the owner of the land. It is for him and his friends to enjoy. In the Galatians passage, the Holy Spirit is described as a tree growing in a believer's life and producing a variety of fruit. That fruit belongs to the Owner and He shares it with His friends.

For example, who gets the benefit from a manifestation of love in a believer's life? *Others!* Who gets the benefit of longsuffering? *Others!* Who gets the benefit of gentleness? *Others!* Who derives the benefit from goodness? *Others!* How about meekness? It is the same.

Incidentally, note that joy is part of the manifestation in a Spirit-filled life. Being a Spirit-filled Christian is not a morbid, down-in-the-mouth, agonizing experience. Unfortunately, in some reference Bibles there is a marginal note immediately following Ephesians 5:18, breaking the continuity of the thought; however, verses 18 through 21 are all a single sentence and, read in that light, emphasize a truth often missed.

There we are told: "And be not drunk with wine, wherein is excess; but be filled with the Spirit; speaking to yourselves in psalms and hymns and spiritual songs, singing and making melody in your heart to the Lord; giving thanks always for all things unto God and the Father in the name of our Lord Jesus Christ; submitting yourselves one to another in the fear of God." So psalms, hymns, spiritual songs, singing, melody making, praise and thanksgiving are overflow manifestations of the Holy Spirit's fullness in a believer's life.

How logical, therefore, that we find singing and praise at the Gate of the Fountain. In the twelfth chapter of Nehemiah, after the wall had been completed and was dedicated, we are told in verse 27: "And at the dedication of the wall of Jerusalem they sought the Levites out of all their places, to bring them to Jerusalem, to keep the dedication with gladness, both with thanksgivings, and with singing, with cymbals, psalteries, and with harps." Then, after naming many of the singers, priests, Levites and princes, it tells how, "with the musical instruments of David the man of God, and Ezra the scribe before them" (Vs. 36), it was "at the fountain gate" that they "went up by the stairs of the city of David," giving thanks as they went to the water gate (Vss. 37-38), which we will be examining in our next study.

What about the *evidence of the Holy Spirit's fullness for yourself?* Surely the fruit of the Spirit is not personal evidence, since often the Spirit-filled Christian does not realize he possesses the fruit of the Spirit. For example, if he is meek, he does not realize he is meek in the biblical sense of the term. So what personal proof can an individual have?

To put it in the language of our Lord, when He told His disciples about the coming of the Holy Spirit, He said, "He shall glorify me: for he shall receive of mine, and shall show it unto you." This taking of the things of Christ and declaring – announcing, proclaiming, revealing, affirming – them unto you is the evidence of His control in your life.

Somewhere I read of the head of a large Eastern corporation, a Christian man, who felt he could not continue without the fullness of the Holy Spirit in his life. Taking the day off from his work, he set about to seek this fullness.

Someone had told him that if he wanted to be filled with the Spirit, he should read Paul's Epistle to the Ephesians. So, settling comfortably in a living room chair, he turned in his Bible to the Ephesian letter and read it in its entirety. It took perhaps 20 or 25 minutes. He felt no elation or any form of indication that he had been filled.

Someone else had once told him that a good way to get His fullness was to go alone in the country and meditate. So he got into his automobile, drove several miles out into the country, parked his car on a country lane, climbed the fence, and went out into the middle of a field. Seating himself under a large shade tree, he began meditating on the things of God. However, he was convinced that he experienced no fullness of the Spirit.

Returning to his home, he called a close spiritual friend and asked for an appointment. It was already past the noon hour and the friend invited him to meet him at his apartment at five that evening. When he arrived, he told his friend the earnest burden of his heart and what he had already done in seeking the fullness.

He said, "Charlie, I simply can't go on any longer with an ordinary Christian experience. I must have the fullness of the Holy Spirit in my life."

His friend told him to present his need and desire to God, yield himself fully to His will, and simply claim the blessing by faith. Together they dropped to their knees and, after brief but earnest supplication, the burden of prayer was lifted. When they rose from their knees, however, the businessman said to his friend, "Charlie, nothing has broken yet. I still do not have His fullness." He was expecting some great emotional upheaval and nothing of that nature had been experienced.

His friend wisely cautioned him not to base it entirely upon emotion, but to claim by faith God's promise, just as he had in the matter of salvation. He reminded him that salvation is a matter of taking God at His Word and God may or may not accompany that answer with an emotional experience. The businessman returned to his own home, went into his living room and sat down in the same chair where he had sought the Holy Spirit's fullness that morning. His Bible, opened at Ephesians, was still on the stand beside the chair. Picking it up, he began to read the Ephesian letter for the second time that day.

What happened?

The epistle he had read in less than 30 minutes that morning he now discovered was like a new book. He read until the wee hours of the morning and still did not get through the first chapter. It took him days to finish Ephesians. The Holy Spirit was taking the things of Christ and declaring them unto him!

But there is a third phase of evidence that the Holy Spirit has full control in an individual's life, and that is *the evidence from the divine standpoint of view.* I do not mean that God needs proof, since He is omniscient, but I mean that the evidence is not especially directed for others or for you. That evidence of His fullness is in the matter of soul winning. Acts 1:8 says, "But ye shall receive power, after that the Holy Ghost is come upon you: and *ye shall be witnesses unto me* both in Jerusalem, and in all Judea, and in Samaria, and unto the uttermost part of the earth" (emphasis added).

In the next chapter we are told that these disciples "were all filled with the Holy Ghost" (Acts 2:4), and, as a result of Peter's Spirit-anointed preaching, "They that gladly received his word were baptized: and the same day there were added unto them about three thousand souls" (Vs. 41).

In Acts 4:31, when again it speaks of them being filled with the Holy Ghost, we are told "they spake the word of God with boldness." And in Acts 11:24, speaking of Paul's missionary associate, Barnabas, we are told, "he was a good man, and full of the Holy Ghost and of faith: and much people was added unto the Lord." The "much people" being "added unto the Lord" was in direct relation to the fact that he was "full of the Holy Ghost."

Dr. R. A. Torrey, in his book, *The Person and Work of the Holy*

Spirit, tells of a time when, preparatory to the return of Dwight L. Moody to Chicago for special meetings, the ministers were holding noonday prayer sessions at the YMCA. One of the brethren rose to his feet and suggested that what they needed was an all-night prayer meeting of the ministers. Torrey agreed and invited them to meet at the Chicago Avenue Church, of which he was then pastor, the next Friday night at ten o'clock.

When that hour rolled around, there were four or five hundred people gathered at the church, which is now known as The Moody Church. However, Satan obviously did not want any victory won and he did everything he could to destroy the effectiveness of the prayer time. To begin with, three men got down on the floor by the door and began to holler, shout and pound the floor in such a manner that no one else could even think. When a brother went to remonstrate with them and suggest that things be done scripturally (that is, "decently and in order," according to I Corinthians 14:40), they cursed him in reply.

Another man, obviously with mental problems, jumped to his feet and ran into the very center of the group, shouting that he was Elijah. Confusion continued for about two hours and many became discouraged and left. However, some were there for the express purpose of seeking God's blessing and were determined that Satan would not defeat them. It was around midnight when all the hindering forces had been defeated and those who remained got down to serious praying.

Torrey said that for the next two hours there was such praying as he had rarely heard. Then, about two in the morning, the atmosphere became hushed and subdued. No one prayed aloud. There was some soft sobbing, but no audible voices in prayer or even supplication and praise. The very air seemed saturated with the presence of God's sweet Holy Spirit.

What was the result?

One businessman left that prayer meeting and caught an early morning train for Missouri. Arriving at his destination, he transacted his business and then inquired at the hotel if any church were having special meetings. Learning that the Cumberland Presbyterians were having a protracted meeting, he went to their service. Rising to his feet, he asked permission to speak and, when it was granted, spoke with such power that 58 or 59 people were converted to Christ on the spot!

Another businessman left that prayer meeting in the early morning hour and caught a train for Wisconsin. Soon word came back that 38 men and boys had been won to Christ in the city where he ministered. Still another man, a student at the Moody Bible Institute, left that prayer meeting for another section of Wisconsin and Torrey said that almost immediately he began receiving communication from clergymen in the area inquiring about the youth and telling how he had been speaking in schools, jails, the Soldiers' Home, and churches with conversions resulting wherever he ministered.

Torrey went on to say: "In the days that followed, men and women from that meeting went out over the earth and I doubt that if there was any country that I visited in my tour around the world – Japan, China, Australia, New Zealand, India, etc. – in which I did not find someone who had gone out from that meeting with the power of God upon him. For me to doubt that God fills men with the Holy Spirit in answer to prayer would be thoroughly unscientific and irrational. I know He does. And in a matter like this, I would rather have one ounce of believing experience than ten tons of unbelieving exegesis."

He did not mean that experience is better than revelation, but when the Word of God is understood and applied, there will be plenty of biblical experience. The real, true evidence of the Spirit-filled life is not found in emotion, exalted feelings, shakings, speaking with tongues, or other things of that nature – *it is in producing fruit and being occupied with Him!*

Finally, just a word about the question,

III. THE BENEFITS: *What Are the Results of a Spirit-Filled Life?*

A. The Highest Spiritual Stature Possible

In addition to what has already been said, it should be emphasized that here are the highest heights obtainable for any individual in this life. There is nothing greater, as far as earthly experiences are concerned, than the fullness of the Holy Spirit in a believer's life.

We have been calling attention in these messages to the progressive nature of the gates. Right here at the Gate of the Fountain is the climax of a believer's status before God. The remaining four gates in the Jerusalem wall have to do with things and events rather than our personal responsibilities before God. This, then, is the peak, the mountaintop. How we should seek and strive for the Spirit-filled life!

B. Doing Greater Works Than Christ

Or, to put it another way, the result of the Spirit-filled life is doing greater works than even Christ performed during His earthly ministry. This is an amazing but scriptural statement that no one should dare make without the clear teaching of the Word of God to back it up. Jesus Himself said, "Verily, verily, I say unto you, he that believeth on me, the works that I do shall he do also; and **greater works than these** shall he do; because I go unto my Father" (John 14:12, emphasis added).

How is this possible? The key is in the context. Note the last clause of the verse, which states the condition, "because I go unto my Father." Then, in verses 16 and 17, He explained, "I will pray the Father, and he shall give you another Comforter, that he may abide with you forever; Even the spirit of truth ... "

In short, it is only through the Holy Spirit's fullness that we can do the "greater works" than Christ!

C. Leadership in Life, in Service

God guides! That is one of His promises for those who walk with Him and are filled with His Spirit. The Psalms, for example, are full of it: "Lead me, O Lord, in thy righteousness" (5:8). "He leadeth me beside the still waters ... he leadeth me in the paths of righteousness" (23:2, 3). "Lead me in thy truth, and teach me" (25:5). "... for thy name's sake lead me, and guide me" (31:3). "I will instruct thee and teach thee in the way which thou shalt go" (32:8). "For this God is our God for ever and ever: he will be our guide even unto death" (48:14). "Thou shalt guide me with thy counsel, and afterward receive me to glory" (73:24). "If I take the wings of the morning, and dwell in the uttermost parts of the sea; even there shall thy hand lead me, and thy right hand shall hold me ... lead me in the way everlasting" (139:9-10, 24).

Over a half-century ago, when I pastored in the county seat town of Graham, Texas, we used several of the Moody Institute of Science films, created, directed and narrated by Irwin Moon, the son of a man I later met while preaching at the Calvary Baptist Church in downtown Los Angeles – a popular, soul-winning, dedicated layman everyone called "Daddy Moon." On one occasion we even rented the Graham city auditorium to present one of the Moody Science films.

Dr. Moon, in one of those productions, told an amazing story of the incredible guidance system God installed in the salmon. While there are different species of salmon (we think here of the Pacific Chinook Salmon, ranging in size from 15 to 25 pounds), everyone, I suppose, is familiar with how these amazing fish, spawned in fresh water, go down the Columbia River (or whatever stream is near their birthing place), enter the Pacific Ocean, go to wherever they go – often, scientists tell us, traveling thousands of miles – then return to the same spot from whence they came, sometimes jumping large waterfalls to get back to exactly where they were spawned.

In this film, Dr. Moon told of a salmon bred in a Northern California hatchery that was released into a small channel, entered a stream, then a river, then the Pacific Ocean. After traveling thousands of miles, it headed for home. He said the salmon found the river where it had entered the ocean, swam to the stream and then the exact channel from whence it came. Then it not only swam up that inlet, but somehow managed to work its way up the drain, go up a 3-foot pipe going straight up, and push through a heavy screened lid to reach the tank where it was spawned!

"Incredible," you say? That's an understatement.

Who told that fish where to go? *God!* Who needs to tell you were to go and how to get there? *The same God!* He makes no mistakes and when you follow the leading of His Holy Spirit, you cannot go wrong!

An Old Testament example of this relates to Abraham's servant, Eliezer of Damascus, who went to find a bride for Isaac. He made the choice a matter of prayer and when God led him to Laban's house and his beautiful daughter, Rebekah, he gave thanks to God, saying,

"Blessed be the LORD God of my master Abraham, who hath not left destitute my master of his mercy and his truth: *I being in the way, the LORD led me* to the house of my master's brethren" (Genesis 24:27, emphasis added). Just as the Spirit of Jehovah led Eliezer, so He leads those who wait upon Him for His direction, especially those "in the way," those who are doing His bidding.

Permit a personal example here. When the writer pastored the Temple Baptist Church in Portsmouth (OH), I was doing visitation late in the afternoon. As was my usual custom, I had my visits lined up like ducks in a row, so I would not waste time. Everything was fine until I got to my last visitation card, a few miles past the area where I was visiting.

What should I do? It was getting late and these folks would possibly be sitting down to their evening meal. My own wife and children would be waiting for me. Yet I felt so strongly that I should make my final scheduled call that I drove on to their home in the country. As I feared, they were seated at the table, having already started to eat.

I tried to excuse myself, saying I would come back another day. But, no, the man insisted and his wife agreed, coming to the living room and sitting down to talk. The blessed Holy Spirit opened the conversation well and in no time I was explaining why they needed to be saved and exactly how it could take place.

To make a long story short, both trusted Christ and I left them rejoicing in what they had done. They planned to make their profession public two days later in church and present themselves for believer's baptism.

Alas, between then and Sunday the wife suddenly took sick and before they could make it to church, she went to Heaven. A week or so later I baptized the grieving widower alone.

I still rejoice, when I think about it today, that I followed the leading of the Holy Spirit and made one more visit that afternoon, even though it was late and seemingly an untimely occasion.

Conclusion

The Niagara Falls, in addition to being one of the world's great honeymoon attractions for newlyweds, is one of America's most vivid examples of power. Its tremendous flow of water, averaging about 194,940 cubic feet per second – coupled with its steep drop – has resulted in major hydroelectric projects by both Canada and the United States, supplying power for entire cities.

Yet even this flow of mighty power can be – *and has been* – stopped. On the night of March 29, 1848 Niagara Falls shut down completely. Those of us who have been near the Falls know that the tremendous roar of its action can be heard for miles away. On this night it became as quiet as a walk in a cemetery at 3 a.m., causing people to rush from their homes in amazement. Some were convinced the end of the world was taking place and others ran to the shores of the Niagara River to investigate for themselves.

It seems, as was reported later, a heavy wind had activated tons of ice that, in turn, had jammed the river's entrance near Buffalo. For approximately 30 hours this non-human dam blocked the flow of water. Eventually, the wind and ice shifted again, the ice dam was broken, and citizens once again began hearing the familiar roar of the falls.

Have you had a spiritual Niagara stoppage in your service for Christ? While once the power of Almighty God was flowing in your life, this is no longer true. You are like the son of the prophet who was working with Elisha on a new dormitory when his ax head flew off and landed in the Jordan River (II Kings 6:1-7). You are now just flailing away with the cutting edge of your service gone.

Is that true? Have you lost – or never experienced – this Gate of the Fountain encounter in your life and service? Our purpose in this message has been two-fold: (1) give you a proper understanding of the Spirit-filled life; (2) create a desire within you to live that type of life. Thank God, He *can* and *will* fill all who will permit Him to do so!

If you stand on the deck of a great ocean-going liner at midday and look at the water, you will see the reflection of the sun. If you row a small boat out into the middle of a shallow lake or pond, you will see the reflection of the same sun. Stand beside a tiny mountain spring, perhaps no more than a foot in diameter, and you will see the reflection of that same mighty sun. Or, rising early in the morning, you will find the same sun reflecting from a tiny dewdrop on the lawn.

The sun has a way of adapting itself with regard to its reflection. No ocean is too big to receive it, nor is a dewdrop too small! Thus it is with a believer and the Holy Spirit. Regardless of a man's capacity – whether it is like an ocean, a lake, a mountain spring, *or a dewdrop* – God is able to fill him!

"And be not drunk with wine, wherein is excess; *but be filled with the Spirit*" (Ephesians 5:18, emphasis added).

Another Niagara story was told by Charles Haddon Spurgeon. He said a boat carrying two men was overturned on the river above the falls and they were being swept toward certain death. Someone on shore managed to float a rope to them and they eagerly grasped it. Shortly a huge log floated by them and because it was so much bigger, one of the men loosed his grip from the rope and laid hold of the wood.

You know what happened. The man holding on to the rope was dragged to the shore and saved, while the man clutching the log went over the falls and perished. What was the difference? One had a firm connection to the shore and one did not. So with people today who are in danger of eternal damnation. The rope of faith is anchored in Heaven; the logs of ritualism, works and all forms of human effort are not.

If you have never yet received the Lord Jesus Christ as personal Savior, by faith receive Him at once. The Scripture expresses it: *"But as many as received him, to them gave he power to become the sons of God, even to them that believe on his name"* (John 1:12). The moment you are willing to receive Him by faith, that moment you will become His child and Heaven will be yours!

Chapter 8

THE WATER GATE!

"Moreover the Nethinims dwelt in Ophel, unto the place over against the water gate toward the east, and the tower that lieth out.

"After them the Tekoites repaired another piece, over against the great tower that lieth out, even unto the wall of Ophel."

– Nehemiah 3:26, 27

The application for this gate in the experience of the Christian is the blessed Word of God. In Scripture, water is used frequently as a symbol of God's written Word, the Bible. Note these examples:

"Husbands, love your wives, even as Christ also loved the church, and gave himself for it; that he might sanctify and cleanse it with the **washing of water by the word**' (Ephesians 5:25, 26, emphasis added).

"Now ye are **clean through the word** *which I have spoken unto you"* (John 15:3, emphasis added).

"Wherewithal shall a young man **cleanse his way? By taking heed thereto according to thy word**' (Psalm 119:9, emphasis added).

Then there is the classic example of our Lord explaining the new birth to Nicodemus in John 3. He warned him, "Verily, verily, I say unto thee, Except a man be born again, he cannot see the kingdom of God. Nicodemus saith unto him, How can a man be born when he is old? can he enter the second time into his mother's womb, and be born? Jesus answered, Verily, verily, I say unto thee, **Except a man be born of water** and of the Spirit, he cannot enter into the kingdom of God" (Vss. 3-5, emphasis added).

Two elements are necessary in this spiritual birth, one is spiritual "water" and the other is the Holy Spirit. What is this water of the new birth? Peter tells us, *"Being born again, not of corruptible seed, but of incorruptible,* **by the word of God**, *which liveth and abideth for ever"* (I Peter 1:23, emphasis added). The water is the Word!

We are told that the Nethinims "dwelt" [lit., *lived*] at the Water Gate. Who were the Nethinims? Well, the name in Hebrew literally means "dedicated ones," appointed ones. According to *The New International Dictionary of the Bible*, they were "temple servants, mentioned only in the later books of the OT. In a sense, all the Levites were Nethinim (Num 8:19), for they were given by the Lord as a gift to Aaron and his sons for the divine service." Ezra 8:20 tells us, "of the Nethinims, whom David and the princes had appointed for the service of the Levites, two hundred and twenty Nethinims: all of them were expressed by name," returned with him to Jerusalem from the Babylonian captivity.

Those dedicated servants who are going to work for Him need an abundance of the water of the Word of God! It is a vital essential in their ministry if they are going to succeed in fulfilling His will.

Everyone is familiar with the mention of the Water Gate in Nehemiah 8 because it is a favorite of those who insist expository preaching is the *only* kind – and we certainly agree with its value and importance, even though this is the only case they can find in all 66 Books of the Bible. There we find that Nehemiah read the book of the law "and gave the sense."

Alas, this may not be expository preaching after all – in which case there would be *no* example in Scripture. The new *Holman Christian Standard Bible* translates this verse, "They read the book of the law of God, translating and giving the meaning so that the people could understand what was read." Since the people assembled came from all over – and many could not understand Hebrew – it was primarily a "translating" and "paraphrasing" of the passages into the language of the people. That was probably the "gave the sense" of which Scripture speaks.

The Water Gate is mentioned there by Nehemiah. It says "all the people gathered themselves together as one man into the street that was before the water gate" (Vs. 1). *Why?* To demand that Ezra the priest "bring the book of the law of Moses, which the LORD had commanded to Israel" [the Word of God] and read it to them. "So they read in the book in the law of God distinctly, and gave the sense, and caused them to understand the reading" (Vs. 8). They returned the next day and Ezra again read to them from the Word of God, "even to understand the words of the law" (Vs. 13). This continued throughout the Feast of Tabernacles, "Also day by day, from the first day unto the last day, he read in the book of the law of God" (Vs. 18).

The reading, explaining and understanding *resulted in obedience.* As Nehemiah tells us, they did what the Word said "because they had understood the words that were declared unto them" (Vs. 12). This sums up beautifully what the Water Gate is all about: *reading, interpreting, understanding, obeying the Word of the Living God!*

There is an impressive children's song written by Mike and Ruth Greene that goes like this:

> Obedience is the very best way
>   To show that you believe.
> Doing exactly what the Lord commands
>   Doing it happily.
> Action is the key. Do it immediately.
>   Joy you will receive.
> Obedience is the very best way
>   To show that you believe.
>
> We want to live pure, we want to live clean
>   We want to do our best.
> Sweetly submitting to authority
>   Leaving to God the rest.
> Walking in the light, keeping our attitude right,
>   On the narrow way;
> For if we believe the Word we receive,
>   We always will obey."
>
> [Copyright, 1977, by Musical Ministries, used by permission]

Let's learn some lessons from the Water Gate in Christian experience. For one thing,

I. THE PERFECTION: *It Is a Gate Needing No Repairing!*

We find it highly significant that, of all the gates mentioned in this chapter, this is the only one where there is no mention of *building* or *repairing.* By way of example, "they builded the sheep gate" (Vs. 1), "the fish gate did the sons of Hassenaah build" (Vs. 3), "the old gate repaired" (Vs. 6), "the valley gate repaired" (Vs. 13), "the dung gate repaired" (Vs. 14), "the gate of the fountain repaired" (Vs. 15), but the Water Gate was a place where the servants of the Lord "dwelt."

This was certainly no oversight or error on the part of the scribe, but an evidence of the guiding hand of the Spirit of the Living God in preparing the record. The only mention of repair relates to the section *beyond* the Water Gate, by the Tekoites, and has to do with the wall, not the gate.

Truly, *the Word of God needs no repairing!*

This is so in spite of the strong, violent and vitriolic attacks of its enemies for literally thousands of years, using their heaviest artillery. We think of the assaults of Thomas Paine, Francois Marie Arouet Voltaire, Robert Green "Boasting Bob" Ingersol, Bertrand Russell, Herbert George "H. G." Wells, Julian Sorell Huxley, and others too numerous to mention. They have come and gone; the Word of God remains!

Its enemies have tried to disprove it *scientifically*, and met with failure in every effort. One by one, as science makes further advances, the alleged discrepancies between it and biblical statements disappear into the sunset.

Its enemies have tried to disprove it *historically*, and met with failure in every effort. What critics have claimed to be errors in history evaporate when more evidence is obtained. It seems as if each pick of the archaeologist's spade uncovers new evidence to show the Word of God correct and the critics wrong.

Its enemies have tried to disprove it *a thousand and one other ways*, and met with failure in every effort. Thank God, the self-appointed critics have been unable to put a single dent in the dear old Water Gate. As John Clifford wrote so beautifully with both wit and wisdom:

> Last eve I stood beside the blacksmith door
> And heard the anvil ring the evening chime,
> And looking in, I saw upon the floor
> Rude hammers worn with beating years of time.
> "How many anvils have you had," said I,
> "To wear and batter all these hammers so?"
> "Just one," said he, with a twinkling of the eye,

"The anvil wears the hammers out, you know."
"So," said I, "The anvil of God's Word
For centuries critics' blows have beat upon,
And still the sound of falling blows is heard,
But the anvil is unharmed, the critics gone."

The Word of God needs no repairing despite being written so long ago, by so many different scribes, coming from such different walks of life. Its first book was probably written at least 3,500 years ago. Its history dates back an estimated 6,000 years. At least 40 different penmen put down what the Spirit of God instructed, men from entirely different backgrounds and temperaments: kings and commoners, farmers and fishermen, priests and prophets, warriors and politicians, self-taught and highly educated – *yet all writing in perfect harmony!*

It is never out-of-date. Other books are discarded frequently as new information is uncovered. In our public schools, new textbooks need to be written every year or so, especially in areas of science – *but not so with the Word of God!*

Years ago, when the writer's library was destroyed in a church fire, the insurance company wanted to reimburse with a few cents on the dollar, saying books have no value after being read once (which is true of fiction, no doubt), and that all data is in a state of flux. I had to argue that mine were reference works in a field where the data remains constant and normal insurance values do not apply.

No, the Bible is never out-of-date. It is still the world's best seller, the most widely read of all literature among mankind. It still has a living, vital message for all classes of men, women and children, of all lands, and all languages. Statesmen, scientists, scholars and others of this sort do well to ponder its pages and obey its precepts, just as do the children, the uneducated and other commoners.

There is no need to bring the Bible up-to-date, to repair it. "The law of the Lord is perfect" just as it is, even as David declared it to be in his day (Psalm 19:7). Nothing needs to be added, nothing it says needs deletion, and nothing needs correction or changing. It alone can meet the longings and needs of hungry, hurting souls. No so-called New Theology or Social Gospel can ever do this.

And, thank God, *it will continue to stand for ever!* Isaiah 40:8 expresses it: "The grass withereth, the flower fadeth: but the word of our God shall stand for ever." And our Lord Jesus Christ promised, in Mark 13:31, "Heaven and earth shall pass away: but my words shall not pass away." *Hallelujah!*

II. THE PARALLEL: *It Is a Gate Closely Connected to the Fish Gate!*

When we were examining the second gate, the Fish Gate, listing the ones who worked in that area, we discovered, "And next unto them the Tekoites repaired; but their nobles put not their necks to the work of their Lord" (Vs. 5). The Fish Gate, remember, spoke of soul winning, fishing for men. Now, at the Water Gate, we find the Tekoites again, this time repairing the section of the city wall right beside it (Vs. 27).

What does this tell us? Simply that soul winning and the Word of God are inseparable. One cannot be an effective winner of souls without careful and expert use of God's Word. Exciting and thrilling stories, personal testimonies, illustrations and allegories all have their place, perhaps, but it is the Word of God that gets the job done. "The law of the Lord is perfect, *converting the soul*" (Psalm 19:7*a*, emphasis added).

One reason we have so many spiritual miscarriages in our churches lies in the careless manner some workers handle the "deliveries," failing to properly use the Word of God. Yet a new birth is utterly impossible apart from the life-giving Sacred Scripture. Note some Bible statements, with emphasis added, to this effect:

"So then faith cometh by hearing, **and hearing by the word of God**" (Romans 10:17).

"Of his own will begat he us **with the word of truth**, that we should be a kind of firstfruits of his creatures" (James 1:18).

"Being born again, not of corruptible seed, **but of incorruptible, by the word of God**, which liveth and abideth for ever. ... And this is the word which by the gospel is preached unto you" (I Peter 1:23, 25).

How is this possible? "For the word of God is quick [lit., *living*] and powerful, and sharper than any two edged sword, piercing even to the dividing asunder of soul and spirit, and of the joints and marrow, and is a discerner of the thoughts and intents of the heart" (Hebrews 4:12). "Is not my word like as a fire? saith the LORD; and like a hammer that breaketh the rock in pieces?" (Jeremiah 23:29).

Notice next,

III. THE PAUSE: *It Is a Gate to Stop and Meditate!*

As we have already noted, the Nethinims "dwelt" there. At all the other gates discussed thus far, there was "building" and "repairing," terms of intense activity. At the Water Gate, the emphasis is placed by the Holy Spirit on dwelling, *a description of passivity, of inaction.* The term "dwelt" is the Hebrew word, ϑασηαβ, and is used throughout the Old Testament to signify sitting down or resting. It is the same word used in Psalm 23:6 to describe the saint's final resting place in Heaven, "... and I will **dwell** in the house of the LORD for ever."

Pausing and meditating at the Water Gate results in joy and blessedness! The psalmist said of the "blessed" man: "His delight is in the law of the LORD; and in his law doth he meditate day and night. And he shall be like a tree planted by the rivers of water, that bringeth forth his fruit in his season; his leaf also shall not wither; and whatsoever he doeth shall prosper" (Psalm 1:2, 3). What a beautiful picture of delight and sweetness!

As this psalm also indicates, pausing and meditating at the Water Gate results in spiritual success. When Joshua took over the job Moses failed to accomplish – and was about to cross the Jordan River at flood stage to begin the conquest of Canaan – he was assured by Jehovah God: "Only be thou strong and very courageous, that thou mayest observe to do according to all the law, which Moses my servant commanded thee: turn not from it to the right hand or to the left, that thou mayest prosper whithersoever thou goest. This book of the law shall not depart out of thy mouth; but thou shalt meditate therein day and night, that thou mayest observe to do according to all that is written therein: for then thou shalt make thy way prosperous, and then thou shalt have good success" (Joshua 1:7, 8).

We could learn a lesson here from Mary, the mother of Jesus. Many events took place at the time of our Lord's birth that were difficult to understand or explain. For example, after the announcement of

Messiah's birth was made to the shepherds watching their flocks and they came to the stable at Bethlehem to see Him, making known abroad their experiences, Luke tells us, "And all they that heard it wondered at those things which were told them by the shepherds" (2:18).

Not so, Mary! The beloved physician informs his readers in the next verse, *"But Mary* KEPT *all these things, and* PONDERED *them* IN HER HEART" (emphasis added). She meditated on them.

Later in the chapter, Luke describes the family trip to Jerusalem for the Feast of the Passover when Jesus was 12 years old. Starting back to Nazareth where they lived, it was discovered that Jesus was not in the caravan. They returned to Jerusalem seeking Him and, after three days, found Him in the temple, "sitting in the midst of the doctors, both hearing them, and asking them questions, and all that heard him were astonished at his understanding and answers" (Vss. 46, 47).

When Mary rebuked Him for His actions that had caused them so much grief, He responded, "How is it that ye sought me? wist ye not that I must be about my Father's business?" (Vs. 49). Yet, Luke again tells us, "They understood not the saying which he spake unto them" (Vs. 50). And once again the beloved physician adds, *"... but his mother* KEPT *all these sayings* IN HER HEART" (Vs. 51, emphasis added).

Her example is a good one to follow, especially when you find things in the Bible you do not understand. Don't *disbelieve* them; *meditate* upon them. The more you meditate and pray over Scripture, especially after you have repaired the Gate of the Fountain, the more understanding you will receive and the greater your faith will become. That is why the Bible so frequently speaks of "meditating day and night" on what is written. *It works!*

We could also learn a lesson by considering the contrast made by Christ between the two sisters, Mary and Martha. Luke 10:38-42 is a passage that has perplexed many because of the seeming rebuke our Lord gave to one who was busy serving Him. Here is the story:

> *"Now it came to pass, as they went, that he entered into a certain village: and a certain woman named Martha received him into her house.*
> *"And she had a sister called Mary, which also sat at Jesus' feet, and heard his word.*

"But Martha was cumbered about much serving, and came to him, and said, Lord, dost thou not care that my sister hath left me to serve alone? bid her therefore that she help me.

"And Jesus answered and said unto her, Martha, Martha, thou art careful and troubled about many things:

"But one thing is needful: and Mary hath chosen that good part, which shall not be taken away from her."

What was our Lord saying to Martha? Didn't He want her service? Is the incident implying that it is wrong to lovingly wait on Him and attend to His needs?

Of course not!

Think about it. What was Mary, who had "chosen that good part," doing? While Martha was "cumbered" [Greek, περισπω, "in the sense of being over-occupied about a thing"] with "much serving," Mary was sitting at Jesus' feet, listening to "His word." In 21st century phraseology, we would say she was reading her Bible, listening to the Word of God, thus having fellowship with Almighty God.

That is more important to Him than our service. In fact, He does not want service that is not preceded by fellowship, reading our Bible (Him talking to us), and praying (our talking to Him). If we are too busy serving Him to read our Bibles and spend time in prayer, we are simply too busy – far busier than God ever intended us to be!

More than that, service apart from such fellowship with Him will be barren and fruitless. That is why He warned in John 15:5, "I am the vine, ye are the branches: He that abideth in me, and I in him, the same bringeth forth much fruit: *for without me ye can do nothing*" (emphasis added).

Did you ever use sympathetic ink? More commonly known as invisible ink, you can write a lovely letter with it, admiring your precise penmanship, meticulous logic, and the magnificent prose with which you express your sentiments. However, unlike ordinary ink, which you can easily read when you are finished, sympathetic ink leaves nothing but a blank paper.

That is what service for Christ is when performed outside of intimate fellowship with Him. There is nothing lasting by way of result.

There is often a lot of sound, a lot of show, a lot of activity, but no substance – nothing that meets the "eternity" test. It takes heat to bring the ink to light again. And the "revealing fire" of the Judgment Seat of Christ will bring out the true character of such service for all to see.

There is another application to sympathetic ink, fortunately. Often people come to the pages of the Old and New Testaments, claiming to see nothing of value or help – failing to understand the message. But the child of God who will approach even the most difficult passages – *such as Peter wrote about in II Peter 3:15, 16* – with careful meditation and study, asking the blessed Holy Spirit to perform His holy task as Teacher, He will add His fire to those pages and the thoughts which were invisible will come to light, clearly and helpfully.

Finally, in considering the Water Gate, note,

IV. THE PROFIT: *It Is A "Profitable" Gate!*

We are thinking here of Paul's declaration to the young preacher: "All scripture is given by inspiration of God, and is profitable for doctrine, for reproof, for correction, for instruction in righteousness: that the man of God may be perfect, throughly furnished unto all good works" (II Timothy 3:16-17).

Two indisputable facts are stated here: (1) **ALL** Scripture is given by God; (2) **ALL** Scripture is profitable. Regarding the latter, four things of profit are listed:

First, it is profitable *for doctrine.* This means that the Word of God is beneficial for discovering the mind and plan of Almighty God. As the believer digs into the Bible he learns truth relating to both God and man that comes from Deity Himself.

Second, it is profitable *for reproof.* This means the Bible is valuable for convicting the erring Christian of his wrong, pointing out how heinous his sin really is in the eyes of a holy God, and warning of its consequences.

Third, it is profitable *for correction.* Here the plan of God is revealed to show the sinning saint how to remedy the problems in his life, get him restored to fellowship with God, and back into business for God.

Fourth, it is profitable *for instruction in righteousness.* This points out the value of God's Word to train us in righteousness, "that which is right." It would not be enough to show us where we were wrong – or even how to get right – if it did not reveal how we could stay right.

In short, the Word of God is profitable for all purposes of the Christian life and walk. It is centered in making us complete: "that the man of God may be perfect, throughly furnished unto all good works" (Vs. 17). Perfection here does not carry the thought of sinlessness, but the idea of maturity. It is through His Word that Christians can develop mature, godly characters.

Even more, the Bible is profitable to keep us from falling into sin. Psalm 119:11 highlights this truth: "Thy word have I hid in mine heart, that I might not sin against thee." Herein lies the difference between the worldling and the Christian. One has his treasures in jewels *without* him (houses, automobiles, bank accounts, stocks and bonds, etc.), while the other has his treasures in jewels *within* him (Holy Spirit, Word of God, etc.). As another has noted about the statement in Psalm 119:11, "Here we have the best thing in the best place for the best purpose."

In short, the Word of God is profitable for gaining victory over Satan. When our Example was tempted of the devil in the wilderness during that period of 40 days and 40 nights, in every single case where the details are given, our Lord answered the tempter, "*It is written ...*" (Vss. 4, 7, 10), gaining the victory through the Word of God.

Does Satan appeal to the lust of the flesh after Jesus has been without food for nearly six weeks, urging Him to turn stones to bread, gratifying that desire in a way His followers could not, through a miracle? Then the Master answers, "*It is written,* Man shall not live by bread alone, but by every word that proceedeth out of the mouth of God," quoting Deuteronomy 8:3.

Does Satan appeal to the pride of life, taking Him up into the holy city and setting Him on a pinnacle of the temple, high above the Kidron Valley, with the challenge to claim Psalm 91:11-12, jumping off and letting the angels bear Him up in their hands? Then the Master responds, "*It is written again,* Thou shalt not tempt the Lord thy God," this time quoting Deuteronomy 6:16.

Does Satan appeal to the lust of the eyes, taking Him to a high mountain and showing Him the kingdoms of the world with all their glory, assuring Him that if He will fall down and worship him He can have them at once, by-passing the agony of the cross? Then the Master answers, "*It is written*, Thou shalt worship the Lord thy God, and him only shalt thou serve," now quoting from Deuteronomy 6:13.

Are we stronger or smarter than our Master? Of course not! If He needed to rely on the Word of God for victory over Satan, can we obtain it some other way? Is there a shortcut, an easier method for us? Perish the thought! His every answer, His every defense was from the Word of God. Ours cannot, *must not* be less.

This is a truth learned by the Christians to whom John wrote: "... I have written unto you, young men, because ye are strong, and the word of God abideth in you, and ye have overcome the wicked one" (I John 2:14). And it is a truth the tribulation saints will learn at a great price: "They overcame [Satan] by the blood of the Lamb, and by the word of their testimony; and they loved not their lives unto the death" (Revelation 12:11).

Conclusion

Dear Christian, how "oft used" is the Water Gate in your life? Our Lord, in answering the religious leaders of His day about His witnesses, challenged them, "Search the scriptures; for in them ye think ye have eternal life; and they are they which testify of me" (John 5:39).

That challenge has never been annulled. He still cries to one and all today: "Search the Scriptures! *Search the Scriptures!* **Search the Scriptures!**"

Some have. In Acts 17, after Paul and Silas left Thessalonica in the middle of the night because of the opposition of the Jews in that city, they came to Berea and went to their synagogue to herald Messiah's coming to the Jewish population there. Verse 11 tells us, "These were more noble than those in Thessalonica, in that they received the word with all readiness of mind, and searched the scriptures daily, whether those things were so." No wonder "many of them believed" (Vs. 12).

Why should we search the Scriptures daily? A good reason is established in II Timothy 2:15, "Study to show thyself approved unto

God, a workman that needeth not to be ashamed, rightly dividing the word of truth."

In my book, *The Wonder of the Word of God*, I noted that the Princeton University Press had published a book not one person in all the world could read. Titled "The Pylos Tablets," it consists of a transcript of a message written in an unknown, dead language on a clay tablet discovered in some Grecian ruins by archaeologists. The Press printed it, according to director Herbert Bailey, in the hope that some scholar or group of scholars would eventually be able to decipher it.

How like the Bible in the eyes of many people! Scores and scores of people to whom I have witnessed have complained, "I've tried to read the Bible and I can't understand it."

Believe it or not, however, that is what the Bible says about itself in I Corinthians 2:14, "The natural man [that is, *man in his natural state*] receiveth not the things of the Spirit of God: for they are foolishness unto him: neither can he know them, because they are spiritually discerned." No one can hope to understand – apart from the simple plan of salvation – Bible truth, which is spiritual, until he is *born* of the Spirit and receives the *mind* of the Spirit. Then all the "mind of Christ" (Vs. 16) is available to him.

If you do not yet know Him as Lord and Savior, He promises, in John 5:24, "Verily, verily, I say unto you, He that heareth my word, and believeth on him that sent me, hath everlasting life, and shall not come into condemnation; but is passed from death unto life." And Romans 1:16 adds, "I am not ashamed of the gospel of Christ: for it is the power of God unto salvation to every one that believeth; to the Jew first, and also to the Greek."

Trust Him today, *without delay!* Then enjoy and delight in the benefits of the Water Gate.

Chapter 9

THE HORSE GATE

"From above the horse gate repaired the priests, every one over against his house."

– Nehemiah 3:28

This gate received its name because it was "the way by which the horses came into the king's house" (II Kings 11:16), and its application in Christian experience may be determined by the scriptural usage of the 'horse.' For example, in that classic confrontation of Job by Jehovah God, the Almighty asked: *"Hast thou given the horse strength? Hast thou clothed his neck with thunder? Canst thou make him afraid as a grasshopper? The glory of his nostrils is terrible. He paweth in the valley, and rejoiceth in his strength; he goeth on to meet the armed men. He mocketh at fear, and is not affrighted, neither turneth he back from the sword. The quiver rattleth against him, the glittering spear and the shield. He swallowth the ground with fierceness and rage, neither believeth he that it is the sound of the trumpet. He saith among the trumpets, Ha ha; and he smelleth the battle afar off, the thunder of the captains, and the shouting"* (Job 39:19-25).

The horse, according to this vivid description, is a biblical picture of warfare, of fierce and raging conflict. Other passages agree. For example, Proverbs 21:31 says, "The horse is prepared against the day of battle, but safety is of the Lord."

Warfare was the theme in Jeremiah 8:15-17, where we are told: *"We looked for peace, but no good came; and for a time of health, and behold trouble! The snorting of his horses was heard from Dan: the whole land trembled at the sound of the neighing of his strong ones; for they are come, and have devoured the land, and all that is in it; the city, and those that dwell therein. For, behold, I will send serpents, cockatrices, among you, which will not be charmed, and they shall bite you, saith the LORD."*

Later in the book, Jeremiah quotes Almighty God on His judgment against Babylon, telling God's people, *"Thou art my battle ax and weapons of war: for with thee will I break in pieces the nations, and with thee will I destroy kingdoms; and with thee will I break in pieces the horse and his rider; and with thee will I break in pieces the chariot and his rider"* (51:20-21).[1]

Associating horses with warfare is especially true when mentioned in prophecy. In Revelation 6, four horses are specifically described and interpreted for us, all having to do directly with battle or the result of warfare. Verse 2 says, "And I saw, and behold a white horse; and he that sat on him had a bow; and a crown was given unto him; and he went forth conquering and to conquer." Verse 4 tells us, "And there went out another horse that was red; and power was given to him that sat thereon to take peace from the earth, and that they should kill one another; and there was given unto him a great sword." And verse 8 adds, "And I looked, and behold a pale horse; and his name that sat on him was Death, and Hell followed with him. And power was given unto them over the fourth part of the earth, to kill with sword, and with hunger, and with death, and with the beasts of the earth." While verses 5 and 6, describing the black horse, refer primarily to food shortages and famine, let's not forget "an army marches on its stomach" and this is a very vital part of warfare.

Later in the Book of the Revelation of Jesus Christ, beginning the description of the return of our Lord at the time of His revealing, the second phase of His second coming, John tells us, "And I saw heaven opened, and behold a white horse; and he that sat upon him was called Faithful and True, and in righteousness he doth judge and make war" (19:11). Those returning to this earth with Him are described: "And the armies which were in heaven followed him upon white horses, clothed in fine linen, white and clean" (Vs. 14). Christ and all of His redeemed followers are described as riding white horses into battle.

In Joel 2, that famous chapter on which Peter based his sermon at Pentecost, we find, "The appearance of them is as the appearance of horses; and as horsemen, so shall they run. Like the noise of chariots on the tops of mountains shall they leap, like the noise of a flame of

---

[1] There is an interesting aside here. Some men occasionally – foolishly and wickedly in my judgment – refer to their wives in a derogatory sense as "my old battle ax," but God uses it here in a very loving sense, a powerful instrument in His hand for victory!

fire that devoureth the stubble, as a strong people set in battle array"
(Vss. 4-5).

In the Babylonian siege of Jerusalem during the reign of King
Zedekiah, one of that nation's darkest days, God used His prophet
Jeremiah to assure Israel that there would be a national restoration to
the land (Jeremiah 32). This new beginning would follow a tremendous defeat of her enemies, a time of great joy and blessing (Vss. 7-
14), and a time when God would write His law in their hearts (Vss.
31-34). In summing up that victory, Jeremiah wrote, "And the whole
valley of the dead bodies, and of the ashes, and all the fields unto the
brook of Kidron, **unto the corner of the horse gate toward the east**,
shall be holy unto the LORD; it shall not be plucked up, nor thrown
down any more for ever" (Vs. 40, emphasis added).

When Athaliah "destroyed all the seed royal of the house of
Judah" and declared herself to be the new ruler, the youngest son of
King Ahaziah, Joash, was snatched and hidden by his elder sister
Jehoshabeath. After six years, she and others brought Joash into the
house of God and declared him king. It is significant where this
usurper, Athaliah, was judged: "Then Jehoiada the priest brought out
the captains of hundreds that were set over the host, and said unto
them, Have her forth of the ranges: and whoso followeth her, let him
be slain with the sword. For the priest said, Slay her not in the house
of the LORD. So they laid hands on her; and when she was come to
the entering of **the horse gate** by the king's house, **they slew her
there**" (II Chronicles 23:14-15, emphasis added). Victory over the
evil Athaliah took place at the Horse Gate.

And, remember, the 21st chapter of Proverbs ends with the words:
"The **horse** is prepared against **the day of battle**: but safety is of the
LORD" (Vs. 31, emphasis added).

While other illustrations might be given, these should suffice to
establish the point. Just as the ass and the dove are biblical emblems
of peace, so the horse is a scriptural symbol of warfare. And, believe it,
Christians are in the battle of the ages – now nearing its culmination.

In talking to one of my neighbors after the 2004 presidential elec-
tion, she explained that she had voted for John Kerry because, "I
don't like war." No one does. However, war is a necessary fact of life
and sometimes it is the best way for saving lives in the long run. The

father of our country, President George Washington said, "To be prepared for war is one of the most effectual means of preserving peace."

Talking about physical warfare, World War II hero General George Patton said, "Wars may be fought with weapons, but they are won by men. It is the spirit of the men who follow and of the man who leads that gains the victory." The same is true in spiritual warfare, although "the weapons of our warfare are not carnal, but mighty through God to the pulling down of strong holds" (II Corinthians 10:4). We need great men and women of faith in this warfare today.

Not only are the children of God a kingdom of priests (I Peter 2:5, 9; Revelation 1:5-6) – and it is significant that the priests were repairing this gate; they are mentioned at only two others, the Sheep Gate where the High Priest and his brethren labored; and the Gate of the Fountain, speaking of the Spirit-filled life, both where spiritual leaders would be expected – but soldiers as well.

There are battles to be fought in the Christian life and victories to be won. As Jude explained: "Beloved, when I gave all diligence to write unto you of the common salvation, it was needful for me to write unto you, and exhort you that ye should earnestly contend for the faith which was once delivered unto the saints" (Vs. 3).

Does it not also seem significant that the Horse Gate comes so late in the progressive order of Christian experience? One is not properly prepared to fight in the Christian army, apparently, until matters of salvation, doctrine, humility, purity, the fullness of the Holy Spirit, and saturation/familiarity with the Word of God are settled. Only then will the Christian's warfare be effective. While a new convert is ready to win souls as soon as he is saved – the Fish Gate immediately followed the Sheep Gate, remember – doing battle for Christ is a horse of a different color, if you'll forgive the pun.

What are some of the characteristics of a good soldier?

I. TAKING ORDERS: *A Good Soldier Must Be Obedient!*

It is not necessary for one to be in the military to realize and acknowledge that an effective army must be a well-disciplined unit. Every soldier cannot be "doing his own thing." There is a proper chain of command and each member of the army is under orders to the one above him in rank – all the way to the top! Only the Commander-in-Chief is exempt.

You see, God is a God of order. Paul, talking about the exercise of spiritual gifts in the church, argued in I Corinthians 14:33, "God is not the author of confusion, but of peace, as in all churches of the saints," then added in verse 40, "Let all things be done decently and in order." This cannot be accomplished unless orders are obeyed; order is impossible apart from obedience.

There is an old Army joke about there being three ways to do something: the *right* way, the *wrong* way, and the *Army* way. Perhaps so, but the spiritual soldier who wants to be effective and successful will do it the Army way, exactly as his Lord commands.

Christians have the example in this of their Commander-in-Chief. Philippians 2:5-8 tells us: "Let this mind be in you, which was also in Christ Jesus; Who, being in the form of God, thought it not robbery to be equal with God; but made himself of no reputation, and took upon him the form of a servant, and was made in the likeness of men; and being found in fashion as a man, he humbled himself, and became obedient unto death, even the death of the cross." One could not find a more thorough example of humble obedience than this manifestation of servitude on the part of our Master in His humanity.

Obedience was the dominant principle of His earthly life. Read the Gospel of Mark, which presents Him as Servant. Listen to His testimony in John 6:38, "I came down from heaven, not to do mine own will, but the will of him that sent me." Hear Him again in Hebrews 10:7, "Then said I, Lo, I come (in the volume of the book it is written of me) to do thy will, O God." And in Hebrews 10:9, "Then said he, Lo, I come to do thy will, O God."

He is our Model for obedience.

Obedience is Linked Inseparably with Blessing!

In the military, obedience is honored with promotion while disobedience results in being stripped of rank. The same is true biblically in spiritual warfare.

Look at Noah! Four times in Genesis 6 and 7 we read that Noah did "according to all that God commanded him." What was the result when Noah did all God directed him: God made him the new father of the human race, supplanting Father Adam.

Look at Abraham! Hebrews 11:8 tells us, "By faith Abraham, when he was called to go out into a place which he should after receive for an inheritance, obeyed; and he went out, not knowing whither he went." What was the result when "Abraham ... obeyed"? God made him the father of His chosen people, Israel.

Look at King Saul! He was commanded by the Lord, in fulfillment of a divine promise dating back to the days of Moses, to "go and smite Amalek, and utterly destroy all that they have, and spare them not; but slay both man and woman, infant and suckling, ox and sheep, camel and ass" (I Samuel 15:3). Saul took an army of 210,000 men and did *nearly all* he had been commanded – most of us would have called it obedience, probably – except he spared *one* man, King Agag, and kept the best of the sheep and oxen for sacrifice to Jehovah, certainly a noble thought. But God called the whole thing *disobedience!*

The Prophet Samuel explained to Saul: "Hath the Lord as great delight in burnt-offerings and sacrifices, as in obeying the voice of the Lord? Behold, to obey is better than sacrifice, and to hearken than the fat of rams. For rebellion is as the sin of witchcraft, and stubbornness is as iniquity and idolatry" (Vss. 22-23). That was wickedness with a capital "**W**."

What was the result of Saul's disobedience? God told him, "Because thou hast rejected the word of the Lord, he hath also rejected thee from being king" (Vs. 23). When those whom God has placed in authority can no longer obey orders, for whatever reason, He removes them from their position of leadership.

Remember also, obedience to His Word is better than all your sacrifices of money, dedicated service, or giving of time to His causes. Obedience brings blessing; disobedience brings loss. As Proverbs 10:8 expresses it, "The wise in heart will receive commandments; but a prating fool shall fall."

Obedience Is by Faith!

We have already seen that "by faith Abraham ... obeyed." This is a vital principle of spiritual life and warfare. Hebrews 11:6 explains,

"But without faith it is impossible to please him; for he that cometh to God must believe that he is, and that he is a rewarder of them that diligently seek him." *Faith is a must!*

There must be *faith in the Commander!* No army ever went anywhere or did anything of note without faith in its leader. This same principle applies in the Christian life, not only with reference to our Commander-in-Chief, but in relation to our churches and church government. There must be complete confidence in the leadership of the man God has placed over the people.

This, obviously, is not the kind of blind faith manifested by disciples in a Jim Jones Kool-Aid situation, but people who do not have respect *for* and confidence *in* their undershepherd will not see many victories in their churches. Failure in many, many church situations is found right here: a lack of confidence in the leadership.

There must be *faith in the victory!* Expect to win! John put it like this: "For whatsoever is born of God overcometh the world, even our faith" (I John 5:4). This great truth was personalized by William Carey, the ex-shoemaker and cobbler who is remembered as the father of modern missions, when he challenged the missionary-indifferent ministerial assembly of his day with his famous sermon on Isaiah 54:2, using the motto for which he became noted: *"Expect Great Things from God. Attempt Great Things for God."*

Again,

II. TRAINING: *A Good Soldier Must Be Thoroughly and Properly Prepared!*

It costs literally thousands upon thousands of dollars for every young man and young woman Uncle Sam trains in the military. Why not just send our youth overseas in times of conflict without training, and save all that money? The answer lies in the fact that it would be foolish suicide for the soldier and wicked homicide for Uncle Sam. It is far wiser – *and cheaper in the long run* – for the government to train its soldiers, considering all the money expended thusly a wise investment.

For the same reason, it is of utmost importance that Christian soldiers be properly trained. When this preacher was a young seminarian there was considerable talk among his peers about quitting school.

The world was going to Hell in a hand-basket and Jesus might return for His own at any moment. None of us would live very long anyway, so why waste time in seminary? Why not get out in the spiritual battlefield immediately and start winning souls?

This argument, frankly, was impressive and seemed to carry considerable weight. Fortunately, most of us rejected it for the same reasons outlined two paragraphs above; the time and money spent in training would pay big dividends in the long run. The wood cutter who spends 30 minutes honing his double-edged ax before entering the forest will cut far more timber in a day than the man who rushes into the woods without taking the time to sharpen it first.

But what do we mean by thorough and proper training?

The Teacher, the Trainer: **GOD!**

Jehovah taught David to war. His testimony is in Psalm 144:1-2: "Blessed be the Lord my strength, which teacheth my hands to war, and my fingers to fight; my goodness, and my fortress, my high tower, and my deliverer; my shield, and he in whom I trust; who subdueth my people under me."

God knows everything that will ever come up in our warfare – *and trains us for it!* That is one reason, unlike Uncle Sam's training of his men, no two warriors are trained by God in exactly the same way. One will have a warfare on the backside of the desert, another will battle in prison, another will have a ministry reaching intellectuals, another may work in a rescue mission, another will fight for truth and righteousness in politics – the list is endless. How wonderful that our sovereign Lord knows the areas where we will be ministering, *and trains us accordingly!*

Our Teacher has never lost a battle and He never will. He has behind Him the experience of thousands of years and hundreds of thousands of engagements. He is the one who led Israel through battle after battle and from victory to victory. The only times Israel suffered defeat was when she disobeyed Him and He did not fight in her behalf.

He knows all the "in"s and "out"s of warfare. He has confronted every possible type of military problem in the spiritual realm – and has emerged from each and every one of them gloriously victorious. *What a Teacher!*

The Text Book: THE BIBLE!

The Word of God sometimes teaches us by illustration and example. Paul referred to some Old Testament people and events, then said, "Now these things were our examples, to the intent we should not lust after evil things, as they also lusted" (I Corinthians 10:6). He added some other incidents, then said again, "Now all these things happened unto them for ensamples; and they are written for our admonition, upon whom the ends of the world are come" (Vs.11).

We can learn from the mistakes of former soldiers such as Moses, David, Samson, Peter, Jonah – and even such pitiful failures as Lot. That is one reason God put their stories in our Bible. At the same time, we can profit and learn from the obedience and success of warriors like Joshua, Gideon, Paul, Abraham and Daniel.

The Word of God does not only teach us by illustration, however, but through direct command as well. To offer but one passage, Ephesians 6 describes in some detail the armor we are to wear into battle, the foes we will face, and the divine secrets for emerging victoriously.

Training by Practical Experience: **PRE-COMBAT!**

Uncle Sam, after giving his recruits the head knowledge needed, takes them out into the field for training in mock battles. These "on the job" experiences sometimes mean the difference between life and death to the soldiers, the margin between success and failure, victory or defeat.

This is why any Bible school or seminary worth its salt has rigorous practical work departments. A head knowledge is not enough; mere book learning does not suffice. Our Lord's disciples spent over three years traveling with Him, getting their practical experience under His watchful eye and careful tutelage. It also shows the advantage of a seminary graduate working on the staff of a successful church before going out on his own to do battle against the wiles of the devil, as Paul's warfare passage describes it (Ephesians 6:11).

Since most Christians will not attend special schools for special preparation, another aid for young Christians in pre-combat training relates to monitoring by an older, experienced child of God. Some churches are good in such discipling of new converts, but the majority have nothing of this kind for their people. Dawson Trotman saw the need during World War II and the Navigators organization was the result.

Perhaps, for the average Christian, this pre-combat experience is most effective in our individual lives. Until we experience victory in our *personal* battles, we cannot hope to have success in our conflicts with the world, the flesh, and the devil.

III. TOUGHNESS: *A Good Soldier Must Be Able to "Take It" As Well as "Give it!"*

God's army is no place for panty-waists, mama's boys, sissies, weaklings, namby-pambies, cream puffs, Little Lord Fauntleroys, and the like. As Paul put it in II Timothy 2:3 "Thou therefore **endure hardness**, as a good soldier of Jesus Christ" (emphasis added).

Be Able to Take Persecution and Tribulation

While these are feared by most, they actually benefit us. They make us stronger. Romans 5:3-5 says: *"Not only so, but we glory in tribulations also; knowing that tribulation worketh patience; and patience, experience; and experience, hope; and hope maketh not ashamed; because the love of God is shed abroad in our hearts by the Holy Ghost which is given unto us."* In short, tribulations and persecutions are heavenly blessings. Disguised at the time they are experienced, perhaps, but blessings nonetheless.

They cause the true soldier to become stronger. One of my personal friends in the armed forces wrote me to report his observation that one of two things happened to those in his company who professed to be Christians when they left home. Either they lost out entirely and dropped any profession of Christ and Christianity, or they became stronger spiritually than ever before. No lukewarm Christian can stand up against the forces Satan wages against him in the armed services. The persecution there separates the true from the false, the men from the boys – building up and strengthening the true.

Be Able to Take Chastisement!

We use the word chastisement here in the biblical sense of discipline, not necessarily punishment. There are two main reasons for scriptural chastening in God's Army: (1) not obeying orders; (2) to make the person a better soldier.

In this light, no wonder we read Proverbs 3:11-12, "My son, despise not the chastening of the Lord, neither be weary of his correction; for whom the Lord loveth he correcteth, even as a father the son in whom he delighteth."

In that great chastening passage of Hebrews 12:5-15, the apostle quotes these verses from Solomon and then tells us God chastens us "for our profit, that we might be partakers of his holiness" (Vs. 10). Such is part and parcel of our training.

While it is true that a soldier in God's Army must be able to take it, it is equally true,

IV. TENACIOUSNESS: *A Good Soldier Must Also Be Able to "Give It!"*

Being a soldier in the Lord's army is a "never turn back, never retreat" proposition. The battle cry is, as described in some of the old hymns of the faith: "ONWARD, Christian soldiers, ONWARD"; it is "THE FIGHT IS ON, O Christian soldier."

In spiritual warfare it is true that a good offense is the best defense. This is often the experience of reality whether in sports, the army, or in Christian service.

The noted Methodist hymnist, Charles Wesley, put it:

> Soldiers of Christ, arise And put your armor on,
> Strong in the strength which God supplies Thru His eternal Son;
> Strong in the Lord of hosts, And in His mighty pow'r:
> Who in the strength of Jesus trusts Is more than conqueror.

Stand then in His great might, With all His strength endued,
And take, to arm you for the fight, The panoply of God;
That having all things done, And all your conflicts past,
Ye may o'ercome through Christ alone And stand entire at last.

Leave no unguarded place, No weakness of the soul;
Take ev'ry virtue, ev'ry grace, And fortify the whole.
From strength to strength go on, Wrestle and fight and pray;
Tread all the pow'rs of darkness down,
And win the well-fought day.

Conclusion

Oh, dear Christian, the Horse Gate is a vital one in your Christian experience. Be constantly on your guard against the enemy. Satan and his evil forces are going to be your daily combatants, seeking to defeat and destroy your testimony for Christ.

Not infrequently his gang arrives on the battlefield dressed as angels of light. Paul warned of this in II Corinthians 11:14-15, after describing deceitful workers who transform themselves into the apostles of Christ, saying, "And no marvel; for Satan himself is transformed into an angel of light. Therefore it is no great thing if his ministers also be transformed as the ministers of righteousness; whose end shall be according to their works."

"Fight the good fight of faith ..." (I Timothy 6:12). "Thou therefore endure hardness, as a good soldier of Jesus Christ. No man that warreth entangleth himself with the affairs of this life; that he may please him who hath chosen him to be a soldier" (II Timothy 2:3, 4).

Ignore the advice of the world's Norman Vincent Peales, Robert H. Schullers, and other so-called positive thinkers. Conflict and negativism *are* important. Don't sidestep the Horse Gate in your Christian experience! If you do, you'll not win the crown He intended for you.

Chapter 10

THE EAST GATE

"After them repaired Zadok the son of Immer over against his house. After him repaired also Shemaiah the son of Shechaniah, the keeper of the east gate. After him repaired Hananiah the son of Shelemiah, and Hanun the sixth son of Zalaph, another piece. After him repaired Meshullam the son of Berechiah over against his chamber."

– Nehemiah 3:29, 30

It was a sad day for Israel – and for the world – when the glory of the Lord departed from the Temple in the City of Jerusalem. Its escape route can be traced in the Book of Ezekiel, starting with the third verse of the 9th chapter: *"And the glory of the God of Israel was gone up from the cherub, whereupon he was, to the threshold of the house."*

From over the mercy seat in the Holy of Holies to the threshold, spilling over until it filled the court, then "the glory of the LORD departed from off the threshold of the house, and stood over the cherubims. And the cherubims lifted up their wings, and mounted up from the earth in my sight; when they went out, the wheels also were beside them, and every one stood **at the door of the east gate of the LORD'S house**; and the glory of the God of Israel was over them above" (10:18, 19, emphasis added).

After hovering for a brief time over the East Gate, we next read: "Then did the cherubims lift up their wings, and wheels beside them; and the glory of the God of Israel was over them above. And the glory of the LORD went up from the midst of the city, and stood upon the mountain which is **on the east side** of the city" (11:22-23, emphasis added). Thus the Shekinah glory of Jehovah disappeared from the temple, from the city of Jerusalem, from Israel, and from the earth.

The thing to note here is that *it departed from the East Gate!*

The next reference relates to God's Shekinah glory returning in Ezekiel 43:1-5. After recording his magnificent vision of the new temple, the prophet tells us: "Afterward he brought me to the gate, **even**

the gate that looketh toward the east; and, behold, the glory of the God of Israel **came from the way of the east;** and his voice was like the noise of many waters; and the earth shined with his glory. And it was according to the appearance of the vision which I saw, even according to the vision that I saw when I came to destroy the city; and the visions were like the vision that I saw by the river Chebar; and I fell upon my face. And the glory of the LORD came into the house **by the way of the gate whose prospect is toward the east.** So the spirit took me up, and brought me into the inner court; and behold, the glory of the LORD filled the house" (emphasis added).

Once again notice the language about the glory of the Lord returning: "the gate that looketh toward *the east*," "came from the way of *the east*," "by the way of the gate whose prospect is toward *the east*." The next chapter adds, "Then he brought me back the way of the gate of the outward sanctuary which looketh toward **the east**; and it was shut. Then said the LORD unto me; This gate shall be shut, it shall not be opened, and no man shall enter in by it; *because the LORD, the God of Israel, hath entered in by it*, therefore it shall be shut" (44:1-2, emphasis added). In short, the East Gate is the one associated with the return of our Lord; its application in Christian experience speaks of the second coming of Jesus Christ!

The East Gate, of course, faced the rising sun and, in our Christian experience, looks for "the Sun of righteousness [to] arise with healing in his wings" (Malachi 4:2).

Anyone who has ever attended a committal service for a deceased loved one or friend – or who has ever visited a cemetery, for that matter – has observed the fact that all the graves (*even of atheists!*) face toward the east! For centuries there has been a conviction that our Lord will return from the east and His people wanted to be facing in that direction when He did.

The significance of some of the names of the men at this gate harmonizes beautifully with the thought of the second coming. For example, Shemaiah means "heard of the Lord." For nearly 2,000 years His people have been praying, in conformity with His specific instruction, "Thy kingdom come" (Matthew 6:10). Thank God, that petition is going to be answered, perhaps very soon.

Another name associated with this gate is Shechaniah. It means "habitation of the Lord" and signifies the fact that when He returns it will be to receive His own into everlasting habitations, the place He went ahead to prepare for us in fulfillment of His promise in John 14. We will then be with Him, living and reigning with Him forever!

Hallelujah!

Do you need scriptural proof that He is coming again? Listen to the testimony of the angels at the time of His departure into Heaven, following His first coming: "Ye men of Galilee, why stand ye gazing up into heaven? This same Jesus, which is taken up from you into heaven, shall so come in like manner as ye have seen him go into heaven" (Acts 1:11).

Listen to the testimony of the one who described himself "not a whit behind the chiefest apostles," namely, Saul of Tarsus, who was transformed by the grace of God into the Apostle Paul: *"I would not have you to be ignorant, brethren, concerning them which are asleep, that ye sorrow not, even as others which have no hope. For if we believe that Jesus died and rose again, even so them also which sleep in Jesus will God bring with him. For this we say unto you by the word of the Lord, that we which are alive and remain unto the coming of the Lord shall not [precede] them which are asleep. For the Lord Himself shall descend from heaven with a shout, with the voice of the archangel, and with the trump of God; and the dead in Christ shall rise first; then we which are alive and remain shall be caught up together with them in the clouds, to meet the Lord in the air; and so shall we ever be with the Lord"* (I Thessalonians 4:11-17).

If you are still not convinced, listen to the testimony of our Lord Himself: "Let not your heart be troubled; ye believe in God, believe also in me. In my Father's house are many mansions; if it were not so, I would have told you. I go to prepare a place for you. ***And if I go and prepare a place for you, I will come again and receive you unto myself***; that where I am, there ye may be also" (John 14:1-3, emphasis added).

I was on an ordination council one time in Texas and the young ministerial applicant, facing the council of ordained, experienced ministers and scared half to death (as all such individuals are, no doubt), when one of the elders asked what his position was on the return of Christ. He meditated just a moment and then nervously blurted out, *"I'm for it!"*

So are we! To be a little more specific, however, consider first,

I. THE TECHNIQUE: *The Manner of His Coming!*

Let's look at it in the negative first,

What it is NOT

It is not ***death!*** Death is an enemy and second coming of Christ certainly does not fall into that classification for the children of God. We are told in I Corinthians 15:26, "The last enemy that shall be destroyed is death"; and again in verses 54 and 55, "O death, where is thy sting? O grave, where is thy victory? The sting of death is sin; and the strength of sin is the law."

Not only so, but Paul calls death a "departure." In II Timothy 4:6, speaking of his imminent martyrdom by Caesar at Rome, he wrote, "I am now ready to be offered, and the time of my departure is at hand." Yet at the second coming, we do not *go* to Him; He *comes* to us!

Again, the absurdity of thinking the second coming is death can quickly be seen when one substitutes the word 'death" in passages that refer to His return. For example, Titus 2:13 would say, "Looking for that blessed hope, and glorious appearing of DEATH!" *Perish the thought!* And our Lord's response to Peter about whether John would live until Christ returned would become meaningless: "If I will that he live till he die, what is that to thee?" (John 21:22).

We are not sure how many saints around the globe die every second, but if we only counted one, that would be 3,600 "second comings" for Christ every hour, 86,400 "second comings" every day, and 31,536,000 "second comings" every year. This idea moves the thought of His return from the sublime to the ridiculous. No, His coming is not death.

Neither was it ***the coming of the Holy Spirit to indwell believers!*** If that were true, Christ returned as soon as He went away, since He said about the Holy Spirit, "Nevertheless, I tell you the truth; It is expedient for you that I go away; for if I go not away, the Comforter

will not come unto you; but if I depart, I will send him unto you"
(John 16:7).

This, once again, makes a precious promise meaningless. Keep in
mind also that the Acts, all of the Epistles, and the Revelation of Jesus
Christ were written *after* the coming of the Holy Spirit, yet they con-
tain many, many references to the second coming – and each one
refers to it *as future!*

John 14:16 describes the Holy Spirit as a personage distinct from
the Son, "I will pray the Father," Jesus said, "and he shall give you
another Comforter, that he may abide with you forever." If the second
coming of Christ were fulfilled in the coming of the Holy Spirit, what
He would be saying here is that He must *leave* so that He could *come!*
The God who wrote the Bible is more intelligent than that. [By the
way, note the clear reference to the Trinity here: Father, Son,
Comforter (Holy Spirit).]

Nor is the second coming *a spiritual coming to each convert at the
time of his or her conversion!* He is to return "in like manner" (Acts
1:11) as He left and that means it must be a *literal* coming, a *visible*
coming, a *bodily* coming. Does that happen when a sinner comes to
Christ in a salvation experience? Of course not! Too, none of the
many, many other events which the Word of God tells us will take
place at His second coming occur at the time of an individual's conversion.

There are a host of other theories – all having one thing in common
– such as His coming being the spread of Christianity throughout the
world (the more it spreads, the more He comes); it was the destruction of Jerusalem in 70 A.D.; it will be the gradual conversion of the
entire world, which was part and parcel of the mostly abandoned
postmillennial theory; and other equally false, preposterous notions.

And what is the one thing all these explanations have in common?
*They are all man's attempt to evade the clear, positive teaching of our
Lord's actual, literal, bodily, personal, physical return for His own!*

But let's look at the other side of the coin.

What it **IS**

It is a *literal* coming! The only way to make His coming conform to the other theories is by spiritualizing all the passages which deal with it. Doing so would spiritualize much of both Old and New Testaments, something absolutely unwarranted in sane, sensible, biblical hermeneutics. In fact, we would call doing so *downright wicked!* The prophecies concerning Messiah's first coming were ALL *literally* fulfilled. Many of the prophecies concerning His second coming are given side by side in the same passages with those for His first coming, and by every honest rule of biblical hermeneutics *must be* literally fulfilled as well.

It is a **bodily** coming! He is to come again as He went away and He had a physical body at that time, a body of "flesh and bones" (Luke 24:39). It was one that could be felt, handled – as He invited Thomas to do (John 20:27). It was one that could eat and drink, as when He appeared to The Eleven, He ate "a piece of broiled fish and of an honey comb" (Luke 24:42-43). It is true that His was a changed, transformed body, but it was a physical one nonetheless, the same body in which He was crucified on the cross and buried in the tomb. In fact, it still had the discernible imprints of those wounds (John 20:27; Luke 24:40).

It is a **visible** coming! To quote the angels again at the time of His ascension back to Heaven from the Mount of Olives, "...this same Jesus, which is taken up from you into heaven, shall so come in like manner as ye have seen him go into heaven" (Acts 1:11). He is coming back "in like manner" and He was "seen" when He departed.

Obviously, He will be "seen" when He returns; it will be a visible coming. As Revelation 1:7 assures us, "Behold, he cometh with clouds; and every eye shall see him, and they also which pierced him; and all kindreds of the earth shall wail because of him. Even so, Amen." He will be seen by His own *at the rapture*, but also *at the revelation* by the world that rejected and crucified Him.

It is a **two-fold** coming! His first coming covered a period of well over thirty years with many incidents, miracles and other things included. So His second coming will be spread over a period of years with many events and activities incorporated. The first stage of His second coming will be the **rapture** of the saints. At that time He will come *in the air* to catch up His Bride, those who have been redeemed by His precious blood.

The second stage of His coming will be the **revelation** of the Son to the entire world. At that time He will come *to the very earth*, not just in the air, and His feet will stand upon the Mount of Olives – the very spot from which He ascended after His resurrection.

Consider next,

II. THE TIMING: *The Moment of His Coming!*

Unscrupulous preachers have gotten rich pretending to have inside information about this matter, something every good Christian abhors. The trash cans of time are filled with false prophecies by such false prophets who erred in their false predictions. Some of the erroneous dates of the past two centuries include the year from March 21, 1843 to March 21, 1844; October 22, 1844; 1914; 1918; 1920; 1925; 1941; January 7, 1972; 1975; September 11-13, 1988; and 9 a.m. (CST), October 28, 1992. And that is just a sample!

We will simply set forth in Bible terms what God has said about it.

"A Little While"

This is the language our Lord used in John 16:16, "A little while, and ye shall not see me; and again, a little while, and ye shall see me, because I go to the Father," something that perplexed His disciples and caused Him to use the remainder of the chapter to enlarge upon it. In fact, there is still controversy today among His disciples as to whether the two "little while"s separated His crucifixion and His resurrection only, or whether they involve the immediate separation and His second advent.

F. F. Bruce warned, "We should not imagine too quickly that we understand what was so unintelligible to the disciples. It is easy to suppose that Jesus meant, 'In a little while you will not see me, because I am about to die; but in a little while after that you will see me again, because I am going to rise on the third day and appear to you once more.' Certainly he was going to be taken from them in 'a little while' – in a few hours' time – but 'you see me no more' (cf. verse 10) seems to indicate a longer interval than that between

Jesus' arrest and the resurrection appearances. Perhaps, then, it is that 'coming again' promised in John 14:3 that is in view in the words: 'again a little while and you will see me'." *We agree.*

So did the venerable Bishop J. C. Ryle in his classic *Expository Thoughts on the Gospels.* He wrote: "To confine these words to the single point of Christ's approaching death and burial, appears a narrow view of their meaning. Like many of our Lord's sayings on the last evening of His earthly ministry, they seem to extend over the whole period of time between His first and second advents."

Regardless of one's view of "a little while" in John 16, the same identical phrase is unmistakably used in Hebews 10:36-37, where we are told, "For ye have need of patience, that, after ye have done the will of God, ye might receive the promise. For yet a little while and he that shall come will come, and will not tarry."

Yes, He is coming again in "a little while." Remember, please, that the Lord does not reckon time as we do – nor is He bound by our clocks and calendars. In discussing this very subject in II Peter 3, the apostle declared: "Beloved, be not ignorant of this one thing, that one day is with the Lord as a thousand years, and a thousand years as one day." The "little while" has not yet been two full days as a possibility on His calendar.

Perhaps this would be a good place to note that trying to fix the time of His return is totally unscriptural. In fact, it is *anti*-scriptural. Our Lord clearly and emphatically declared to His disciples, when they were pressing Him to reveal the time, "*It is not for you to know* the times or the seasons which the Father hath put in his own power" (Acts 1:7, emphasis added). He narrowed it down even finer when He warned them at the time of His Olivet Discourse, "Of that day and hour knoweth no man, no, not the angels of heaven, but my Father only" (Matthew 24:36). How clearly He declared that we cannot know the time, not the hour nor the day – that secret is locked in the bosom of *the Father!*

Many men have made fools of themselves – and embarrassed the cause of Christ tremendously – by seeking "keys" that would give inside information about His coming. In fact, they are still doing it. Sometimes they think they have found the key in the Bible and other times they have sought it in the occult (astrology), or in such secondary sources as the Great Pyramid.

This practice seems to have really gotten out of hand in the past few decades. A friend of ours said a lady wrote him that she had discovered the key to His coming and enclosed an *M&M Plain* candy wrapper as her evidence. She explained that "M" is Latin for 1,000 and two "M"'s would be 2,000. The "plain" was additional proof that it was plain Christ would return in 2,000 years! Then she quoted Acts 2:19 ("I will show wonders in heaven above and in the earth beneath") as confirmation for this "wonder on earth" she had discovered!

Don't laugh; some of the reasoning of today's most popular and oft-quoted prophetic 'experts' is not much better!

Premillennial and Pretribulation

The only major alternative views to premillennial are amillennial and postmillennial. The former requires spiritualizing so much of the Bible that it does not fall into the realm of honest interpretation, in our humble judgment. It boils down to "if God didn't mean what He said, why didn't He say what He meant?"

As for the latter view, after World War I (and then World War II – plus Korea, Vietnam, Gulf War, two Iraq wars, etc.), the postmillennial outlook range went from dismal to absurd – and most scholars have given up on it, although it has recently been making a comeback. We make no apology whatsoever for accepting the premillennial position as being the only *valid* view that fits *all* the requirements.

Remember that the Antichrist will be destroyed at the revelation of Jesus Christ. Second Thessalonians 2:8 says, "And then shall that Wicked be revealed, whom the Lord shall consume with the spirit of his mouth, and shall destroy with the brightness of his coming." There can be no millennium until he has been destroyed, so a postmillennial coming is an impossibility. Why "watch" if He cannot possibly come for at least more than 1,000 years?

Not only so, but Satan must be bound during the millennium. Revelation 20:1-3 tell us: *"I saw an angel come down from heaven, having the key to the bottomless pit and a great chain in his hand. And he laid hold on the dragon, that old serpent, which is the Devil, and*

Satan, and bound him a thousand years, and cast him into the bottom-
less pit, and shut him up, and set a seal upon him, that he should
deceive the nations no more, till the thousand years should be ful-
filled; and after that he must be loosed a little season." Since Satan
is not bound now, amillennialism cannot possibly be true. If Satan is
bound in the bottomless pit now, what more could he do when loosed
than what he is doing now? If he is bound now, who is deceiving the
nations? Obviously, someone is doing an excellent job of it.

The apostles and other disciples in the years immediately following His ascension were eagerly looking for His return in their lifetime.
For example, Paul instructed the Christians in Thessalonica that,
when Christ returned, **"we** which are alive and remain shall be caught
up together with [the dead in Christ] in the clouds, to meet the Lord
in the air; and so shall **we** ever be with the Lord" (I Thessalonians
4:17, emphasis added).

Note the phrase, **"we** which are alive" at His coming. Paul was
expecting to be alive when He returned, as have all instructed saints
throughout the centuries – something absolutely impossible if a mil-
lennial reign must transpire first. Nor does spiritualizing the statements do much to make the problem go away.

Edith S. Bergman put it like this:

> Perhaps today!
> The trump of God shall sound;
> Perhaps today!
> His shout shall pierce the air;
> Oh, blessed hope
> Of all His blood-bought saints;
> His bride shall rise
> To life, eternal, fair.
> Perhaps today!
> Come quickly, blessed Lord;
> Perhaps today!
> I'll meet Thee in the sky;
> I long to join
> The song of twice-born men,
> Forevermore
> To praise Thy Name on high!

During A Time of Great Apostasy

Quite the contrary of the world being converted before He comes, as postmillennialism demands, our Lord indicated the opposite would be true. He summed up His parable of the unjust judge by asking, "Nevertheless when the Son of man cometh, shall he find faith on the earth?" (Luke 18:8). The obvious inference is that faith will be in short supply at that time. *What a tragedy!*

Instead of letting God rule, those will be days in which men and women are concerned only with the temporal, the earthly, the material, and the sensual. It will be as the days of Noah (Matthew 24:37-39), and as the days of Sodom and Gomorrah (Luke 17:28-30). While we think the principal application in these references applies to the suddenness of His coming, the situation and condition of those days should not be forgotten or overlooked.

Peter and Paul both enlarged on the fact that there will be a great falling away from the Truth in the last days. Some men will have a form of godliness, but will deny the power thereof. Preachers will be denyers of His deity, ridiculers of His resurrection, scoffers of His second coming, and spurners of His sacrificial atonement. Paul (I Timothy 4:1-3; II Timothy 3:1-9) and Peter (II Peter 2:1-3; 3:1-2) both hammered home this truth.

Unexpected to Many

The Lord certainly gave repeated emphasis to the fact of being taken by surprise in direct statement and through the parables He told. In the example of the unfaithful servant, He closed by saying, "The lord of that servant shall come in a day when he looketh not for him, and in an hour that he is not aware of and shall cut him asunder, and appoint him his portion with the hypocrites; there shall be weeping and gnashing of teeth" (Matthew 24:50-51). And He concluded His illustration of the 10 virgins with the application, "Watch therefore, for ye know neither the day nor the hour wherein the Son of man cometh" (Matthew 25:13).

The important thing to remember is that *He may come at any moment!* Robert Murray McCheyne, the famous Scotch preacher, is said to have concluded a message on the second coming by asking his congregation if they thought the Lord might come that very night. When they indicated that they did not expect Him that soon, he reportedly leaned over the pulpit and said in soft, solemn, whispered tones, *"In such an hour as ye think not the Son of man cometh."* He was quoting of course, Matthew 24:44, which adds the plea, *"Therefore be ye also ready."*

In this light, blind Fanny Crosby was faithful to ask in the chorus of her "Will Jesus Find Us Watching?"

> O can we say we are ready, brother?
> Ready for the soul's bright home?
> Say, will He find you and me still watching,
> Waiting, waiting, when the Lord shall come?

Conclusion

Who will be taken at His coming? Let's answer this question also by using the exact language of Scripture.

1. *Those who are ready!* Matthew 25:10 says, about the coming of the Bridegroom, "… and they that were ready went in with him to the marriage and the door was shut."

2. *"They who are Christ's!"* First Corinthians 15:23 says, "Every man in his own order; Christ the firstfruits; afterward they that are Christ's at his coming."

3. *Those "in Christ," both dead and alive!* First Thessalonians 4:16-17 say: "For the Lord himself shall descend from heaven with a shout, with the voice of the archangel, and with the trump of God; and the dead in Christ shall rise first; then we which are alive and remain shall be caught up together with them in the clouds, to meet the Lord in the air; and so shall we ever be with the Lord."

Understand clearly, it is not a question of works or degrees of holiness. Those caught up to be with Him at His coming are raptured solely on the basis of their *possession* of spiritual life!

> Caught up! Caught up! No wings required;
> Caught up to Him by love inspired,

To meet Him in the air.
Spurning the Earth with upward bound,
Nor casting a single glance around,
Nor list'ning a single earthborn sound,
    Caught up in the radiant air!

Caught up! With rapture and surprise;
Caught up! Our fond affections rise,
    Our coming Lord to meet.
Hearing the trumpet's glorious sound,
Soaring to the join the rising crowd,
Gazing beyond the parted cloud,
    Beneath His pierced feet!

O blessed! O thrice blessed Word!
To be forever with the Lord
    In heavenly beauty fair!
Up! Up! We long to hear the cry!
Up! Up! Our absent Lord draws nigh!
Yes, in the twinkling of an eye.
    Caught up in the radiant air.

Of all the gates in Christian experience, after salvation, surely the East Gate is the one most eagerly anticipated. Since that is true, it makes this an all-important question of utmost concern: Are *you* ready?

Is He *your* Savior? If you can answer with a positive yes to that, are you, as a Christian, satisfied with your current spiritual status? Are you content with your service, the number of souls you have won to Him, the kind of a life you will have to present to Him at the judgment seat?

Think about it!

Chapter 11

THE GATE MIPHKAD!

"After him repaired Maichiah the goldsmith's son unto the place of the Nethinims, and of the merchants, over against the gate Miphkad, and to the going up of the corner.

"And between the going up of the corner unto the sheep gate repaired the goldsmiths and the merchants."

– Nehemiah 3:31, 32

Is this a mistake? These gates are supposed to be in the progressive order of a Christian's experience. We started with personal salvation through Christ at the Sheep Gate and our last gate, the East Gate, was the second coming. The children of God have already left the earthly scene, their long sojourn is over. John Bunyan's 'Pilgrim' is Home! What in our Christian experience could possibly follow that?

The answer is found in the *meaning* of the word Miphkad. It means "a place of review," or "a place of appointment." The new *Holman Christian Standard Bible*, in fact, translates this, "the Inspection Gate" (Vs. 31). In Nehemiah's time it was undoubtedly a place where the judges of the city assembled to hear the cases of the people being brought before them, handing down their decisions and judgments. In our Christian experience, this is the place where God reviews our lives from the moment of salvation to either death or rapture. It is the final place of appointment for judgment.

This is not the Great White Throne. No, *no!* Christians will never face God at that Throne to answer to Him for sins committed because that is a judgment of condemnation, a place of reviewing immediately prior to being cast into the Lake of Fire. But although there is "no condemnation to them which are in Christ Jesus" (Romans 8:1), and He has "not appointed us to wrath, but to obtain salvation by our Lord Jesus Christ" (I Thessalonians 5:9), it does not mean there will be no facing of God, no answering to Him, no accounting for failures, no judgment of any sort.

Quite the contrary! The Word of God abounds with references to judgment for Christians. Paul refers to those who are "weak in the faith," ones "God hath received," called properly His "servants," people who live and die "unto the Lord" – then declares of these redeemed ones, "... we shall all stand before the judgment seat of Christ," adding, "So then every one of us shall give account of himself to God" (Romans 14:10, 12).

When he was writing to the Corinthians, after describing the desire of Christians to be well-pleasing of Him in their service, Paul explained, "For we must all appear before the judgment seat of Christ; that every one may receive the things done in his body, according to that he hath done, whether it be good or bad" (II Corinthians 5:10). And the closing chapter in the Word of God is plain to point out the promise of Christ, "Behold, I come quickly; and my reward is with me, to give every man according as his work shall be" (Revelation 22:12).

Our Christian experience has not ended until we stand before His Bema Seat, our lives are reviewed, His fire tries "every man's work of what sort it is," and we "receive a reward" or "suffer loss" (I Corinthians 3:13-15). This is what Daniel Webster meant when he replied to a question as to the greatest thought he had ever entertained, by responding, "My personal accountability to God." The Gate Miphkad is the Christians accountability time to Him for the deeds done in the body on earth as a child of His.

Let us note several things about this final gate in our Christian experience.

I. THE MANNER: *The Time of the Judgment!*

It will be the first thing on God's program at His second coming, immediately after the rapture of His church. The very nature and purpose of this judgment demand that it be the first event after His bride is snatched away – some going so far as to say it will be held in the air before the raptured enter Heaven. That may be why the "dead in Christ" are brought with Him when He comes for the "alive in Christ."

At any rate, this is the Bride making herself ready, as outlined in Revelation 19:7, "Let us be glad and rejoice, and give honour to him: for the marriage of the Lamb is come, and his wife hath made herself ready."

Not only will it be immediately following the rapture, it must take place before the millennium – before the reign of Christ on David's throne for 1,000 years. Since the saints are to reign with Him at that time, it is imperative for the judgment to occur first with places and positions of rulership being determined.

Again, the time of the judgment for Christians will be more than 1,000 years prior to the judgment for the unsaved at the Great White Throne, which follows the millennium. There will be no general judgment of saved and lost, no parting of saints and sinners left and right, as the song we sometimes sing unscripturally teaches.

Revelation 20:1-6 makes this fact crystal clear:

> "And I saw an angel come down from heaven, having the key of the bottomless pit and a great chain in his hand. And he laid hold on the dragon, that old serpent, which is the Devil, and Satan, and bound him a thousand years, and cast him into the bottomless pit, and shut him up, and set a seal upon him, that he should deceive the nations no more, till the thousand years should be fulfilled: and after that he must be loosed a little season. And I saw thrones, and they sat upon them, and judgment was given unto them: and I saw the souls of them that were beheaded for the witness of Jesus, and for the word of God, and which had not worshipped the beast, neither his image, neither had received his mark upon their foreheads, or in their hands; and they lived and reigned with Christ a thousand years. But the rest of the dead lived not again until the thousand years were finished. This is the first resurrection. Blessed and holy is he that hath part in the first resurrection: on such the second death hath no power, but they shall be priests of God and of Christ, and shall reign with him a thousand years."

The context goes on to say that Satan will then be loosed, launch another rebellion against the Most High, be defeated, and then cast into the Lake of Fire to remain there forever and ever. Then the Great

White Throne judgment for Christ-rejectors will take place.

Consider next what the judgment for Christians will be like,

II. THE MAKE-UP: *The Nature of the Judgment!*

First, let us strongly emphasize that this judgment is not what we usually think of by the term judgment. This is not bodily punishment, such as sinners will have in the Lake of Fire. Nor is it anything like the horrible outpouring of the pent-up wrath of Almighty God which will befall the earth during the Great Tribulation. No, the only punishment meted out at the Bema Seat will be depriving of rewards, loss of privileges, and denial of honors.

Not a Question of Condemnation for Sin!

That issue was completely, eternally settled for Christians at Calvary. Our Lord promised, in John 5:24, "Verily, verily, I say unto you, He that heareth my word, and believeth on him that sent me, hath everlasting life, and shall not come into condemnation; but is passed from death unto life." This guarantee, incidentally, was made in the very context of the coming judgment for lost sinners.

God, who cannot lie (Titus 1:2), has promised that our "sins and iniquities will I remember no more" (Hebrews 10:17). What thrilling assurance this is of permanent deliverance from judgment! As H. G. Stafford and P. P. Bliss taught us so sweetly to sing:

> My sin — oh, the bliss of this glorious tho't —
> My sin — not in part, but the whole —
> Is nailed to the cross AND I BEAR IT NO MORE,
> Praise the Lord, praise the Lord, O my soul!

It is interesting to contrast Calvary, where our *sins* were judged, with the Bema Seat, where our *works* will be judged. We came to Calvary as lost sinners; we will go to the Bema Seat as saints, those already saved. We came to Calvary to receive grace; we will go to the Bema Seat to receive merit and reward. We came to Calvary with faith as the ground of our salvation; we will go to the Bema Seat with works as the ground for giving us crowns and honors as proof of our faith's reality. We came to Calvary to receive salvation as a present possession; we will go to the Bema Seat to receive rewards and crowns as a future distinction.

Instead of *condemnation*, the question will be *commendation!*

A Judgment of the Believer's Works!

This review will cover the things done in the body from the time of conversion (obviously, nothing acceptable to God could have been done for Christ prior to it) until the time of the rapture or the believer's death, whichever of the two he experiences. Sir James M. Barrie, the Scottish novelist and playwright, once wrote: "The life of every man is a diary in which he means to write one story, and writes another; and his humblest hour is when he compares the volume as it is with what he vowed to make it."

That is not quite true. The most humbling hour will be when he compares the volume with the blueprint of the life God planned for him in eternity past! As Martha Snell Nicholson expressed it, "the plan of my life as it might have been, had He had His way and I see – how I blocked Him here and I checked Him there; and I would not yield my will." Surely there will be a flood of tears in Heaven at that time.

This review at the Bema Seat will be according to the responsibilities and trust committed to the individual. As Jesus explained at the conclusion of His parable about the steward's servant, "For unto whomsoever much is given, of him shall be much required: and to whom men have committed much, of him they will ask the more" (Luke 12:48).

He will not expect as much from the pastor of the 100-member church as He does from the pastor of a 4,000-member congregation. The missionary in a barren wasteland will not be as accountable as the missionary in a populous place where the people were hungry and receptive to the gospel. The vocational pastor who was forced to earn his living on a 40-hour week assembly line will not be as answerable as the preacher who was free all week to evangelize. The 1-talent servant will not be expected to have as much fruit as his 5-talent contemporary.

In his *Lectures to My Students*, Spurgeon told of a man who had preached to many and won numerous souls to Christ, a matter about which he congratulated himself. But one night he had a dream in which an angel revealed to him that none of the honor would be his at the time of judgment. When he inquired who would receive the credit, the angel replied, "That illiterate lay-brother who sits on the pulpit stair and prays for you; he was the means of the blessing."

We think it entirely true that some invalids will receive greater rewards than some preachers, simply because the former were faithful with the talents given them and the preachers were not – and "unto whomsoever much is given, of him shall be much required."

On Queen Elizabeth's "official birthday" some years back, when she conferred honors on a number of her subjects, one was a 60-year-old postman in northern Wales, a fellow with the unroyal name of Jones. Because Jones, who came from a family delivering Welsh mail for 150 years, had "not missed a day's service in 43 years and got the mail through despite snow, storms and floods," the Queen bestowed the British Empire Medal upon him, expressing the gratitude of the nation.

If an earthly majesty would bestow such a superlative honor on a man for faithfulness in so simple a task as delivering the mail, do you not think the Majesty of Heaven will be even more diligent to make certain each of His subjects receives a proper and gracious award for faithful service done in His Name? *Of course He will!*

This review will be according to *quality*, not necessarily *quantity*; it will not be how *much*, but what *kind*. Second Corinthians 3:13 says, "Every man's work shall be made manifest: for the day shall declare it, because it shall be revealed by fire; and the fire shall try every man's work **of what sort it is**" (emphasis added).

In the parable of the talents (Matthew 25:14-30), the servant who only earned two talents received exactly the same reward as the one who had earned five talents. *Why?* Because the one who earned five talents had five talents to work with, while the one who merely earned two talents only had two talents to invest. In other words, both earned 100% on what they had been given, hence their lord rewarded them exactly the same (note the identical wording about the two in verses 21 and 23).

Motive comes under this heading of "what sort it is," too. One can go to a big city and spend a 10-hour day, preaching on street corners, handing out tracts, giving baskets of food to the poor, going door-to-door and witnessing, yet receive small or no reward at the Bema Seat. *Why?* Because the motive behind the service was wrong, such as the praise of men, a mere sense of duty, pride, to impress others, self, or any number of fleshly reasons. You see, God is not fooled about why we do things and at the judgment for Christians it will all come out.

This review will be according to opportunities given. When Mary of Bethany took the "alabaster box of ointment of spikenard very precious; and she brake the box, and poured it on [Jesus'] head," some were filled with indignation, murmuring over what they called "the waste of the ointment." Judas, especially, complained that it should have "been sold for more than three hundred pence, and have been given to the poor."

On the other hand, Jesus responded: "Let her alone; why trouble ye her she hath wrought a good work on me. For ye have the poor with you always, and whensoever ye will ye may do them good: but me ye have not always. She hath done what she could: she is come aforehand to anoint my body to the burying. Verily I say unto you, Wheresoever this gospel shall be preached throughout the whole world, this also that she hath done shall be spoken of for a memorial of her" (see Mark 14:3-9).

That phrase in verse 8 is the key: *"she hath done what she could!"* At the Bema Seat, no one will be judged on the basis of gifts he did not possess or opportunities unavailable to him. Have *you* done what *you* could?

David, the sweet singer of Israel and man after God's own heart wanted to do something he couldn't. What he desired was right and proper – and for God's glory – yet God said no. Solomon referred to it on a festive occasion years later, explaining: "It was in the heart of David my father to build an house for the name of the LORD God of Israel. And the LORD said unto David my father, Whereas it was in thine heart to build an house unto my name, thou didst well that it was in thine heart" (I Kings 8:17, 18).

Note four things here: (1) David wanted to build a magnificent temple for the Name of Jehovah. (2) God forbad it. (3) David gave up the project and died without doing it. (4) The Lord gave David credit for building it because "it was in thine heart."

Here is a young woman with plans to go to Bible school after her high school graduation, eventually going as a missionary to a foreign land. Yet in the summer months between high school and college she is injured in an automobile accident, forced to spend the rest of her life alternating between a bed and a wheel chair, paralyzed from the neck down. Instead of blazing new trails for Christ in another land, she is confined to the walls of her own home, praying for those who are away doing the job she once longed to accomplish. At the Bema Seat she will receive a missionary's reward and be told by her Lord, "Thou didst well that it was in thine heart."

Here is a young man with a burden to proclaim the gospel to the multitudes, but before he can go off to college and receive his training his father is killed on the job. It becomes his lot, as the eldest in a large family, to stay at home and earn the living for his mother and the other children – perhaps even financing *their* educations. Instead of ministering to masses, his preaching is confined to the one-on-one witnessing in his own neighborhood and community. At the Bema Seat he will receive an evangelist's reward, being told by his Lord, "Thou didst well that it was in thine heart."

Here are some of the things for which we will be rewarded:

Faithful stewardship. "Therefore when thou doest thine alms, do not sound a trumpet before thee, as the hypocrites do in the synagogues and in the streets, that they may have glory of men. Verily I say unto you, They have their reward. But when thou doest alms, let not thy left hand know what thy right hand doeth; that thine alms may be in secret: and thy Father which seeth in secret himself shall reward thee openly" (Matthew 6:2-4).

Persecution for Christ's sake. "Blessed are ye, when men shall hate you, and when they shall separate you from their company, and shall reproach you, and cast out your name as evil, for the Son of man's sake. Rejoice ye in that day, and leap for joy: for, behold, your reward is great in heaven: for in the like manner did their fathers unto the prophets" (Luke 6:22, 23).

Loving your enemies, giving to the poor. "Give to every man that asketh of thee; and of him that taketh away thy goods ask them not again. And as ye would that men should do to you, do ye also to them likewise. For if ye love them which love you, what thank have ye? for sinners also love those that love them. And if ye do good to them which do good to you, what thank have ye? for sinners also do even the same. And if ye lend to them of whom ye hope to receive, what thank have ye? for sinners also lend to sinners, to receive as much again. But love ye your enemies, and do good, and lend, hoping for nothing again; and your reward shall be great, and ye shall be the children of the Highest: for he is kind unto the unthankful and to the evil" (Luke 6:30-35).

Willingness in service. "For though I preach the gospel, I have nothing to glory of: for necessity is laid upon me; yea, woe is unto me, if I preach not the gospel! For if I do this thing willingly, I have a reward: but if against my will, a dispensation of the gospel is committed unto me" (I Corinthians 9:16, 17).

Perseverance in ministering. "Call to remembrance the former days, in which, after ye were illuminated, ye endured a great fight of afflictions; partly, whilst ye were made a gazingstock both by reproaches and afflictions; and partly, whilst ye became companions of them that were so used. For ye had compassion of me in my bonds, and took joyfully the spoiling of your goods, knowing in yourselves that ye have in heaven a better and an enduring substance. Cast not away therefore your confidence, which hath great recompence of reward. For ye have need of patience, that, after ye have done the will of God, ye might receive the promise. For yet a little while, and he that shall come will come, and will not tarry" (Hebrews 10:32-37).

A host of other things are promised reward in Scripture, but these are a sampling.

The Bema Seat is also,

A Preparing of the Bride for Marriage to the Lamb!

Just prior to the revelation of the Lord Jesus Christ as KING OF KINGS AND LORD OF LORDS (Revelation 19:11-16), John "heard as it were the voice of a great multitude, and as the voice of many waters, and as the voice of mighty thunderings, saying, Alleluia: for the Lord God omnipotent reigneth. Let us be glad and rejoice, and give honour to him: for the marriage of the Lamb is come, and his wife hath made herself ready" (Revelation 19:6, 7).

According to this passage, the Bride is not ready. To be united to the Lamb she must be pure, spotless, undefiled, immaculate, unblemished – in other words, *perfect*. All the dross and deficiencies must be burned away so that only the hallowed remains. As I Corinthians 3:12-13 say, about the redeemed building on the foundation of Christ: *"Now if any man build upon this foundation gold, silver, precious stones, wood, hay, stubble; Every man's work shall be made manifest: for the day shall declare it, because it shall be revealed by fire; and the fire shall try every man's work of what sort it is."* The Bride's wood, hay and stubble will be consumed; her gold, silver and precious stones will not only remain, they will be perfected.

Some Things Could – *and Should* – Be Settled **NOW!**

We dare not leave the discussion of the Bema Seat's nature without pinpointing the truth that many things in a Christian's life should be taken care of long before he or she ever faces the Master. As Paul told the misbehaving saints at Corinth, guilty of disorders at the Lord's Table: "If we would judge ourselves, we should not be judged" (I Corinthians 11:31). How much better to right wrongs *now* than *then*!

When Dwight Lyman Moody died on December 22, 1899, Reuben Archer Torrey was Superintendent of the Bible Institute of Chicago (now Moody Bible Institute) and pastor of the Chicago Avenue Church (now Moody Church), both founded under the leadership and direction of the dynamic Moody. Thomas DeWitt Talmage, the fiery pulpiteer and author/editor, had just retired from his pastorate at the First Presbyterian Church in Washington, D.C.

Unknown to most people, the two men – both with dominant, unbending personalities – had experienced a falling out some time previously. When Talmage learned of Moody's Homegoing, and knowing that his mantle would fall on Torrey, he immediately sat down and penned him a note. In it, he expressed regret for being such a poor Christian as to allow their differences to separate them for

years, confessed his own fault in the matter, and begged Torrey's forgiveness. No one else, apparently, knew about it.

Years later, when J. Vernon McGee was pastor of the Church of the
Open Door in Los Angeles, where Torrey had gone after leaving the
work in Chicago, he found Talmage's letter in an old file and reported it on his nationwide radio program, "Thru the Bible." We assume
Torrey accepted the apology and made one of his own, so both got it
taken care of prior to the Bema Seat. At least Talmage, we know, got
his part settled here rather than there.

Perhaps there is something in your life that needs attention immediately, judging yourself so you won't be judged.

Finally, let's look at,

III. THE MESSAGE: *The Outcome of the Judgment!*

We have already quoted several of the verses in it, but in order to
have it fresh in our mind, consider again that passage in I Corinthians
3:11-15. Paul wrote: *"For other foundation can no man lay than that
is laid, which is Jesus Christ. Now if any man build upon this foundation gold, silver, precious stones, wood, hay, stubble; Every man's
work shall be made manifest; for the day shall declare it, because it
shall be revealed by fire; and the fire shall try every man's work of
what sort it is. If any man's work abide which he hath built thereupon,
he shall receive a reward. If any man's work shall be burned, he shall
suffer loss; but he himself shall be saved; yet so as by fire."*

The results are two-fold:

Some Will Suffer Loss

Verse 15 warns, "If any man's work shall be burned, he shall suffer
loss ...." Alas, some will weep as they watch nearly an entire lifetime of
works go up in smoke, completely destroyed – wood, hay and stubble.

In this life it happens over and over again. A family is awakened in
the middle of the night. The house is on fire, already a raging inferno.
It is too late to salvage anything and the members of the household
are fortunate to escape alive, even though their night clothes are the
sum total of their possessions saved. Perhaps what went up in smoke

was the labor and accumulation of a lifetime. Not only so, but because of its location out in the boondocks, no company would carry insurance on it.

Such a situation is no more lamentable than the pathetic Christian at the Bema Seat who watches his life's work destroyed by Jehovah's purifying fire of holiness. Yes, some will suffer loss, yet so as by fire.

Remember Lot? He had abandoned Uncle Abraham and everything the latter stood for, apparently, eventually moving down into wicked Sodom and becoming as one of them. While he became a great man in the eyes of his fellow Sodomites, amassing a huge fortune in the process, he lost everything in a single night as brimstone and fire fell from Heaven in a judgment from Jehovah. He suffered loss, yet so as by fire.

We do not think any Christian will lose *everything*, however. In the illustrations above, the burned-out families had the clothes on their backs. Lot and his daughters had the clothes on their backs, too, plus what little they were able to carry out of Sodom when the angels hastened them. And so God, I Corinthians 4:5 seems to imply, will give some kind of reward to *every* Christian.

That verse – and note its highlighting that the East Gate comes before the Gate Miphkad – assures us: "Therefore judge nothing before the time, until the Lord come, who both will bring to light the hidden things of darkness, and will make manifest the counsels of the heart: *and then shall every man have praise of God* (emphasis added)." He will find something of value in every Christian, for which to reward him. Hallelujah, what a Savior!

The other result of the judgment is,

Some Will Receive Rewards!

To quote I Corinthians 3:14 again, "If any man's work abide which he hath built thereupon, he shall receive a reward." Even as that which is false and unworthy is destroyed by fire, so the true and the precious will be made more beautiful by those same flames. His fire will only serve to purify the gold, silver and precious stones.

Five different crowns, wonderful symbols of reward, are listed in Scripture:

The Crown of Rejoicing. This is the soul winner's crown, as Paul declared to his converts in Thessalonica: "For what is our hope, or joy, or crown of rejoicing? Are not even ye in the presence of our Lord Jesus Christ at his coming? For ye are our glory and joy" (I Thessalonians 2:19, 20). He said the same of the souls he had won at Philippi: "Therefore my brethren dearly beloved and longed for, my joy and crown, so stand fast in the Lord, my dearly beloved" (Philippians 4:1).

The Crown of Righteousness. This is for those who are looking, longing and living for Christ's return. Paul, about to be executed in a Roman dungeon for his faith, wrote the young preacher: "I am now ready to be offered, and the time of my departure is at hand. I have fought a good fight, I have finished my course, I have kept the faith: henceforth there is laid up for me a crown of righteousness, which the Lord, the righteous judge, shall give me at that day: and not to me only, but unto all them also that love his appearing" (II Timothy 4:6-8).

The Crown of Life. This is the martyr's crown, one given to those who lose their lives for the cause of Christ, such as my friend Roger Youderian, one of the missionaries – along with Nat Saint, Jim Elliot, Pete Fleming and Ed McCully – viciously hacked to death with machetes by the Auca Indians in Ecuador. Roger not only joined the church I pastored in Long Beach (CA), but taught a young boys' Sunday School class, including my eldest son who is now a powerful preacher of the glorious gospel of Christ.

The Apostle John recorded the words of Savior to the persecuted church at Smyrna: "Fear none of those things which thou shalt suffer: behold, the devil shall cast some of you into prison, that ye may be tried; and ye shall have tribulation ten days; be thou faithful unto death and I will give thee the crown of life" (Revelation 2:10). James described it: "Blessed is the man that endureth temptation: for when he is tried, he shall receive the crown of life, which the Lord hath promised to them that love him" (James 1:12).

The Crown of Glory. This is the crown for faithful pastors, the undershepherds over God's flock. Peter wrote to them: "Feed the flock of God which is among you, taking the oversight thereof, not by constraint, but willingly; not for filthy lucre, but of a ready mind; neither as being lords over God's heritage, but being ensamples to the flock. And when the chief Shepherd shall appear, ye shall receive a crown of glory that fadeth not away" (I Peter 5:2-4).

Other faithful teachers, not just pastors, will receive this crown.

The Incorruptible Crown. This is the victor's crown, the one given to God's noble winners on the field of conflict with Satan. Paul described it in I Corinthians 9:24-27: "Know ye not that they which run in a race run all, but one receiveth the prize? So run, that ye may obtain. And every man that striveth for the mastery is temperate in all things. Now they do it to obtain a corruptible crown; but we an incorruptible. I therefore so run, not as uncertainly; so fight I, not as one that beateth the air; but I keep under my body, and bring it into subjection: lest that by any means, when I have preached to others, I myself should be a castaway."

Will you suffer loss or be rewarded at the Bema Seat? Oh, that all of us might be busy laying up treasure in Heaven, gaining crowns to place in gratitude at our Redeemer's feet. He pleads with His followers, "Lay not up for yourselves treasures upon earth, where moth and rust doth corrupt, and where thieves break through and steal: but lay up for yourselves treasures in heaven, where neither moth nor rust doth corrupt, and where thieves do not break through nor steal: for where your treasure is, there will your heart be also" (Matthew 6:19-21).

It seems wise to close this final study on the gates in Christian experience, especially since it relates to the Judgment Seat of Christ, in the words with which Nehemiah closed his book: "Remember me, O my God, for good" (13:31, *l.c.*).

Conclusion

As noted in this message, there are two separate major judgments. One is for the saved and the other is for the lost. The judgment for Christians, which we have been discussing in this chapter, is the Bema Seat, a judgment of *commendation*. The other judgment, for sinners, is the Great White Throne judgment. It is one of *condemnation*.

At which judgment will you be present to be judged? All will be at one or the other. Which one for you hinges on what you do with God's Son, the Lord Jesus Christ. John 3:16-18 expresses it like this: *"For God so loved the world, that he gave his only begotten Son, that whosoever believeth in him should not perish, but have everlasting life. For God sent not his Son into the world to condemn the world; but that the world through him might be saved. He that believeth on him is not condemned; but he that believeth not is condemned already, because he hath not believed in the name of the only begotten Son of God."*

We cannot close this message without appealing to those who have never trusted Jesus Christ as personal Lord and Savior to do so without delay. The Word of God says, "Behold, now is the accepted time; behold, now is the day of salvation" (II Corinthians 6:2).

Interestingly, this series of gates in Christian experience started at the Sheep Gate, which we learned was salvation based upon the sacrificial work of the Lamb of God, Christ Jesus. There can be no Christian experience until salvation has been received. That is the starting point for every Christian experience.

We do not think it is either accidental nor incidental that the chapter on the gates ends, after speaking of the Gate Miphkad, with a reference to the goldsmiths and merchants repairing this section of the wall "between the going up of the corner unto the sheep gate" (Vs. 32).

In other words, the Sheep Gate is not only the starting point for Christian experience; *it is the finish as well.* All roads in Christianity lead by the cross. The Sheep Gate, speaking as it does of the atonement and salvation through the finished work of Christ, is both the center and the circumference of all Christian experience! As Paul declared in I Corinthians 2:2, "For I determined not to know any thing among you, save Jesus Christ, and him crucified." Christ and His finished work are everything in a Christian's life.

If you have never done so before, receive Christ now! John 1:12 describes the simplicity of it: "But as many as received him, to them gave he power to become the sons of God, even to them that believe on his name." And John 6:37 contains His promise, His guarantee: "... him that cometh to me I will in no wise cast out."

You come!

He'll receive you with the open arms of love! William T. Sleeper expressed it over a century ago:

> "Out of my bondage, sorrow and night, Jesus, I come, Jesus I come;
> Into Thy freedom, gladness and light, Jesus, I come to Thee.
> Out of my sickness into Thy health, Out of my want and into Thy wealth,
> Out of my sin and into Thyself, Jesus, I come to Thee.
>
> "Out of my shameful failure and loss, Jesus, I come, Jesus I come;
> Into the glorious gain of Thy cross, Jesus, I come to Thee.
> Out of earth's sorrows into Thy balm, Out of life's storms and into Thy calm,
> Out of distress to jubilant psalm, Jesus, I come to Thee.
>
> "Out of unrest and arrogant pride, Jesus, I come, Jesus I come;
> Into Thy blessed will to abide, Jesus, I come to Thee.
> Out of myself to dwell in Thy love, Out of despair into raptures above,
> Upward for aye on wings like a dove, Jesus, I come to Thee.
>
> "Out of the fear and dread of the tomb, Jesus, I come, Jesus, I come;
> Into the joy and light of thy home, Jesus, I come to Thee.
> Out of the depths of ruin untold, Into the peace of Thy sheltering fold,
> Ever Thy glorious face to behold, Jesus, I come to Thee."

I beg you in His Name, *please come today!*

Chapter 12

ETERNITY!

"But God, who is rich in mercy, for his great love wherewith he loved us,
"Even when we were dead in sins, hath quickened us togeth-er with Christ, (by grace ye are saved;)
"And hath raised us up together, and made us sit together in heavenly places in Christ Jesus:
"That in the ages to come he might show the exceeding rich-es of his grace in his kindness toward us through Christ Jesus."
                                                    – Ephesians 2:4-7

We have finished our Gateways to Glory and are ready to begin our eternity with Christ. While this is not one of the gates, we thought it would be a blessing to readers to talk about it for just a moment.

Dr. J. B. Rowell, writing in *The Evangelical Christian* well over a half-century ago, in a sermon titled, "The Radiance of Eternity," quot-ed the poem:

> Eternity! Eternity!
> There came there a bird each thousandth year,
> One sand grain from the hills to bear;
> When all had vanished, grain by grain,
> Eternity did still remain.

He went on to give the definition of the Greek word αιονιοσ, mean-ing eternal, as given by the noted Greek lexicographer, Dr. Joseph Henry Thayer: "Without beginning or end, that which always has been and always will be, never to cease, everlasting."

Glory to God, after all the gates of our Christian experience are completed, we will be in His presence for all eternity. This is what the writer of Hebrews referenced when he wrote, *"Wherein God, willing more abundantly to show unto the heirs of promise the immutability of his counsel, confirmed it by an oath: that by two immutable things, in which it was impossible for God to lie, we might have a strong consolation, who have fled for refuge to lay hold upon the hope set before us: which hope we have as an anchor of the soul, both sure and stedfast, and which entereth into that within the veil; whither the forerunner is for us entered, even Jesus, made an high priest for ever after the order of Melchisedec"* (Hebrews 6:17-20).

Will you be in eternity with Christ throughout the ages to come? As we seminarians used to sing on the street corner during our open-air meetings, it is "Heaven or Hell for you and me, where will you spend eternity?" In our evangelistic/expository commentary, *Hebrews: Streams of Living Water*, at the close of the study "Souls Anchored in Heaven," we referred to the sad lines of the illustrious poet, Lord Bryon, who may have been penning his own epitaph:

> There are wanderers o'er the sea of eternity,
>   Whose bark drives on and on,
> And anchored ne'er shall be.

Jude described them this way: "Woe unto them! for they have gone in the way of Cain, and ran greedily after the error of Balaam for reward, and perished in the gainsaying of Core. These are spots in your feasts of charity, when they feast with you, feeding themselves without fear: clouds they are without water, carried about of winds; trees whose fruit withereth, without fruit, twice dead, plucked up by the roots; raging waves of the sea, foaming out their own shame; wandering stars, to whom is reserved the blackness of darkness for ever" (Vss. 11-13).

Surely no one in his right mind would choose Hell and its instability over Heaven and its permanence. Ah, but that is the nature of sin: *insanity!* That is why the Word of God speaks of the lost in such language as "fools" "foolish ones," "senseless," "without knowledge," and "void of understanding."

On the other hand, who could begin to describe the joys and blessings of eternity with Christ? George Milligan, the noted Greek scholar, in *The Ascension and Heavenly Priesthood of our Lord*, commenting about Hebrews 7:25 ("Wherefore he is able also to save them to the uttermost that come unto God by him, seeing he ever liveth to make intercession for them"), called attention to the verb "intercession" (Greek, εντυνψηανω) and noted:

> It is unfortunate that no better translation can be suggested for this word, for we have come to limit the thought of intercession entirely to prayer: while the verb means rather to meet or transact with one person in reference to another. ... In the case of Christ therefore, 'we are to understand it of every act by which the Son, in dependence on the Father, in the Father's name, and with the perfect concurrence of the Father, takes His own with Him into the Father's presence, in order that whatever He Himself enjoys in the communication of His Father's love may become also theirs.' (p.152)

My, the blessing of communication we will have with the Trinity throughout eternity! Who could begin to describe or even imagine it!

John Newton's heart-warming song, "Amazing Grace," originally had at least a dozen stanzas. Some of the lesser known include:

> In evil long I took delight,
>   Unawed by shame or fear;
> Till a new object met my sight,
>   And stopped my wild career.

[This was followed by the verse starting, "I saw One hanging on a tree," then came:]

> Sure, never, till my latest breath
>   Can I forget that look,
> It seemed to charge me with His death,
>   Though not a word He spoke.

> My conscience felt and owned the guilt,
>   And plunged me in despair;
> I saw my sins His blood had spilt,
>   And helped to nail Him there.

> Alas, I knew not what I did,
>   But all my tears were vain;

> Where could my trembling soul be hid,
>> For I, the Lord, had slain.
>
> A second look He gave that said,
>> "I freely all forgive!
> This blood is for thy ransom paid,
>> I died that thou mayest live!"

[Then follow the 3 verses usually starting the song: "Amazing grace, how sweet," "'Twas grace that taught my heart," and "Thru many dangers, toils and snares." The next verses were,]

> The Lord has promised good to me,
>> His Word my hope secures;
> He will my shield and portion be,
>> As long as life endures.
>
> Yes, when this flesh and heart shall fail,
>> And mortal life shall cease;
> I shall possess within the vail,
>> A life of joy and peace.
>
> The earth shall soon dissolve like snow,
>> The sun forbear to shine,
> But God Who called me here below
>> Shall be forever mine.

[Then came that last, wonderful final verse, which hymnologists say may have been written about a century later by an American, John P. Rees.]

> When we've been there ten thousand years,
>> Bright shining as the sun,
> We've no less days to sing God's praise
>> Than when we'd first begun.[1]

In Deuteronomy 34 we have the record of the death of Moses and I call your attention now to just two verses of the story: *"So Moses the servant of the LORD died there in the land of Moab, according to*

---

[1]Apparently B. B. McKinney took some of these unfamiliar verses and put them to music in a song he titled "He Died for Me."

the word of the LORD. And he buried him in a valley in the land of Moab, over against Bethpeor: but no man knoweth of his sepulchre unto this day" (Vss. 5-6).

Notice that phrase in verse 5: "So Moses the servant of the Lord died ... **according to the word** of the Lord." The Hebrew for "word" there is πεη, and it is saying, "Moses the servant of the Lord died ... **from the mouth** of the Lord."

The old Jewish scholars (they have been working on the Old Testament a whole lot longer than evangelical scholars), paraphrased it in days gone by like this: "So Moses the servant of the Lord died ... **from a kiss from the mouth of the Lord."** These Jewish thinkers associated it with Song of Solomon 1:2, "Let him kiss me with the kisses of his mouth." And whether you know it or not, that is where man gets the popular "kiss of death" phrase.

The latter is used in our day by fiction writers and others as something portraying a horrible thought. Yet originally, what a sweet thought it was: the kiss of death, *a kiss from the mouth of God Himself that freed the soul from the bondage of life and allowed him enter the glories and joys of eternity!*

The concept the Jews in Old Testament times had was a beautiful picture of Jehovah God Himself leaning over the battlement of Heaven, kissing His own, then that individual waking up in Glory. *The kiss of death!* Yes, what a beautiful thought it is.

The Christian Laymen's Tract League put out a little card entitled, "The Homeland." Quoting from a beautiful Gospel song, it says,

THINK ...

Of stepping on shore and finding it
    Heaven;
Of taking hold of a hand and finding it
    God's hand;
Of breathing a new air and finding it
    Celestial air;
Of feeling invigorated and finding it
    immortality;
Of passing from storm and tempest to
    an unbroken calm;
Of waking up and finding it HOME!

When we wake up from that kiss of God, what words can describe our new heavenly Home? The first word I suggest to you is,

BEAUTY!

In thinking about this message and of words to describe Heaven, this was the first thought that came to mind. My, how *beautiful* Heaven must be!

God has almost exhausted human language in the Bible to describe Heaven, especially in the closing part of His Book: gates of pearl, streets of gold, and walls of jasper garnished with all manner of precious stones are some of its wonders. And, of course, beauty of this nature requires light striking on it to make it especially beautiful.

The so-called Painted Desert (actually, colored rock) along the Little Colorado River in Arizona, stretching from the Grand Canyon to the Petrified Forest National Park, isn't much if the sun is not shining. The glitter and glory of the scene is brought out by light. If you visit it on a cloudy, sunless day you will be greatly disappointed.

In Heaven there is no need of the sun or the moon since the Lamb is the light. Can you visualize His glory shining continuously on those gates of pearl, streets of gold, and walls of jasper with their precious stones? Yes, how beautiful Heaven must be!

We might illustrate by the Crown Jewels of England. They have an estimated value of £20,000,000 and, at the rate of exchange at the start of this 21st century of $1.50 per £, that would be, in our currency, roughly about $30,000,000. Yet no one much sees them. They are kept in an underground vault at the Tower of London with sixteen Yeoman warders and curators guarding them day and night – in addition to all the electronic protection for those jewels.

Thank God, no one will be hiding the beauty of the glory of Heaven! It will be on exhibit for all the inhabitants to enjoy throughout eternity.

George W. Vanderbilt, who was the grandson of steamboat and railroad tycoon Cornelius Vanderbilt, was riding on horseback in the Blue Ridge Mountains of Virginia over a hundred years ago. He came up over the top of a hill and saw the French Broad River in the valley below and thought the scene was one of the most beautiful sights he had ever beheld. He immediately determined to build a house right there, ending up with a magnificent French chateau. Work was started about 1890 and finished in 1895.

They built a three-mile railroad to the site just to bring in materials and workers. (It was torn out after the workers finished building the house.) They put together a whole town just to house the thousand men and their families who worked on it. They built shops, a railroad station, a church, a brick factory, a sawmill and other things they needed while they worked on the estate – Biltmore, "Lady on the Hill."

What a house it was! It had 250 rooms on a domain of 125,000 acres. Richard Morris Hunt, first American to be awarded the Royal Gold Medal of the Royal Institute of British Architects and the man who designed both the base of the Statue of Liberty and New York's Tribune Building, was commissioned to handle the mansion. Frederick Law Olmsted, who helped design the grounds at the United States Capitol and New York's Central Park, was given the landscaping chores.

The library housed 20,000 volumes and was described as the most pleasant room in the house. The ceiling featured a painting Vanderbilt bought in Italy. (He toured all over Europe trying to find rare paintings, artifacts, and kindred items with which to furnish the house. Among other things, he found and purchased a Chinese chess set that Napoleon played with on St. Helena during his exile.)

There was a sunken area called Palm Court with marble walls and floors. It was furnished with ferns, flowers and palms grown right there on the estate. They had a grand ballroom with a ceiling 70 feet high, yet acoustics were so perfect a man at one end of the great long table could talk to the man at the other end without shouting. There were 80 servants working fulltime in that magnificent manor house.

The first time they were able to have a great celebration in it was Christmas, 1895. Now it is a National Historic Landmark. As a matter of fact, when Vanderbilt died, his widow gave 120,000 of the acres to the United States government and that is now the Pisgah National Forest. But as beautiful as was Biltmore, "Lady on the Hill," what a poor imitation it would be of the beauty of Heaven! Heaven is beautiful beyond the understanding of mortals.

The second word I thought about was,

PREPARED!

Somewhere I read about a little boy whose father and mother visited New York City. Like most tourists to the Big Apple, their sightseeing tour took in the Empire State Building. They got on the elevator and started up. After going up for a while they got off and moved to another elevator. The lad was watching the floors flash by – 50, 60, 70, 80, 90 – and finally he turned to his dad, pulled on his coat sleeve, and asked earnestly, "Dad, does God know we're coming?"

Well, bless your heart, *God knows we're coming!* He not only knows, He is getting everything fixed up, getting everything ready for our arrival.

Do you remember what Jesus said in the 14th chapter of John, verse 2, "I go to *prepare* a place for you?" He said in the next verse, "And if I go and *prepare* a *place for you* ...." Yes, He is fixing it up for us because He knows we are coming.

By the way, our English word "prepare" doesn't necessarily mean "build." It means "to make ready for," "make adaptable," "to arrange." That is exactly the idea of the Greek word, ηετοιμαζω, as well. Our Lord is in Heaven making ready our eternal dwelling place. How wonderful it will be when He, the master interior decorator, finishes it!

I recall one of the houses we purchased when my ministry made us relocate. The house we purchase was almost new – the previous owners had lived in it only a matter of weeks before backing out of the purchase. My wife "prepared" our new home, spending three weeks to do it. She did not "build" it, although she did make a few new things – drapes, curtains and some other decorations. She spent three long, hard weeks fixing it up and did a very fine, beautiful job.

Jesus has been working some 2,000 years – not three weeks – fixing up a place for us! My, the "specials" He must be preparing in His house for our arrival! "In my Father's house are many mansions ... I go to *prepare* ..."; not build (it has already been built), but to fix it up, to make it lovely for us. Can you even begin to imagine what it will be like?

I have a friend in Florida who was born in the Blue Ridge

Mountains – way back in the boonies. He said that when he was a little boy his mother taught him about the power of prayer and he could remember praying that some day he would get to live in a 'painted' house. All the other kids up and down the street in his neighborhood lived in houses that were nicely painted, but they had no paint at all on their house.

What an improvement Heaven is going to be over living in even an elegantly painted house down here. "Prepared" – Jesus will have it beautifully, perfectly prepared!

Another word I'll mention here is,

MUSIC!

We don't know anyone who doesn't like music. Not everyone loves the same kind, of course, and some will only listen to certain styles: gospel, bluegrass, classical, country, western, rock 'n' roll (if this can be called music) – to name a few.

All of these will fade into the limbo of history when compared to the music of Heaven. Since what it will sound like goes beyond the possibility of finite minds to fathom, let's offer a sample as seen in Revelation 5:11-13, *"And I beheld, and I heard the voice of many angels round about the throne and the beasts and the elders: and the number of them was ten thousand times ten thousand, and thousands of thousands; saying with a loud voice, Worthy is the Lamb that was slain to receive power, and riches, and wisdom, and strength, and honour, and glory, and blessing. And every creature which is in heaven, and on the earth, and under the earth, and such as are in the sea, and all that are in them, heard I saying, Blessing, and honour, and glory, and power, be unto him that sitteth upon the throne, and unto the Lamb for ever and ever."*

What a choir! That is a total of one hundred million, plus thousands of thousands. Each singer will be in perfect pitch, no one will be off key. All will be in perfect harmony. Even those who, down here, couldn't carry a tune in the proverbial bushel basket will sound like Jenny Lind, the Swedish Nightingale – *only better!*

When you compare this thought with times you have been blessed by a melodious male quartet, or a harmonious ladies trio, or a gifted soloist – the splendor of it boggles the mind. And in addition to the vocal music will be that of stringed instruments and other instruments blending with the purified voices of the singers. All we can say is, "Wow!"

Another word about Heaven is,

PURITY!

Sin, iniquity, corruption, defilement is everywhere on earth. Can you imagine what it will be like in a place where no sin or sinner can ever enter? Revelation 21:27 describes it: "And there shall in no wise enter into it any thing that defileth, neither whatsoever worketh abomination, or maketh a lie: but they which are written in the Lamb's book of life."

Perfection. *Absolute perfection!*

No one will have to confess a fault or failure to either man or God because there will be no sin to confess. The Apostle John put it like this: *"Behold, what manner of love the Father hath bestowed upon us, that we should be called the sons of God: therefore the world knoweth us not, because it knew him not. Beloved, now are we the sons of God, and it doth not yet appear what we shall be: but we know that, when he shall appear, we shall be like him; for we shall see him as he is. And every man that hath this hope in him purifieth himself, even as he is pure"* (I John 3:1-3). How wonderful to be "just like Jesus" in this area!

This heavenly country is so pure that just thinking about it makes men pure on earth. We will be like our Lord Jesus Christ and since He did not sin, neither will we. Unlike earth, where they are daily – yea, hourly – reports of murders, rapes, robberies, slanders, drunkenness, divorces, fraud, lying, child abuse and other horrors, not one of those will rear its ugly head in Heaven.

What a wonderful place of holiness it will be.

The final word I want to look at here is,

GRACE!

When I thought about Heaven – "beauty," "prepared" – I also thought about "grace." We don't deserve it. We could never merit it. It is *all* of grace.

Fanny Crosby wrote over 8,000 different poems, many of them

made into beautiful hymns and gospel songs. One time, during a conference at Northfield, Dwight L. Moody asked her to give a testimony. She didn't want to at first, but finally consented.

She rose and said, "Of all the poems I have written, one I have never shared with anybody before. It is my own private poem. I call it 'My Soul's Poem.' I will share it with you now for the first time." It was based on Ecclesiastes 12:6 and Revelation 22:4-5. George C. Stebbins later set it to music and it became very popular, still sung enthusiastically today. It goes like this:

> Some day the silver cord will break,
>   And I no more as now shall sing;
> But, oh, the joy when I shall wake
>   Within the palace of the King.
> Some day my earthly house will fall –
>   I cannot tell how soon 'twill be;
> But this I know – my All in All
>   Has now a place in Heav'n for me.
> And I shall see Him face to face,
>   And tell the story – Saved by grace;
> And I shall see Him face to face,
>   And tell the story – Saved by grace.

And that is what it is – *saved by grace!* Heaven? Yes, based on the fact that Jesus Christ came to earth, born of a virgin; went to the cross of Calvary and suffered, died, and made an atonement for our sins; was buried and rose again the third day. He was delivered for our offences, buried, and raised again for our justification (Romans 4:25).

I remember visiting the spot where Christopher Columbus landed in the New World, on the beach at San Salvador. They have a little memorial there. It is not much of a place (this San Salvador is not to be confused with the other Salvador where they killed the American missionaries; this is a different Salvador, in the Bahamas).

Up until the time of Columbus' voyage they didn't know what was on this side of the Atlantic. As a matter of fact, men sailed up and down the Mediterranean Sea and when they came to that narrow opening between Spain and Africa – the Strait of Gibraltar – they stopped. The great Atlantic Ocean was beyond and they didn't think there was anything on the other side. They thought that was it, period. Spain adopted as its motto: *Ne plus ultra*, which is Latin for "nothing beyond."

Then Christopher Columbus came back with his report and the thinking of mankind was revolutionized. At Valladolid, a city north-west of Madrid in North Spain, when he died in 1506, they erected a monument to his memory. It is still there if you want to go see it. The monument shows a lion with his paw hitting that Spanish motto, *Ne plus ultra*. He is striking the *Ne* and it is being shattered to pieces, just leaving *Plus ultra*, which means "more beyond." After Columbus came back from the New World, Spain was forced to change its motto!

Well, up until Jesus came to earth a lot of people thought there wasn't anything beyond the grave, that when man died that was it. But they were forced to change their evaluation when Jesus came back from the grave with His announcement that there truly is "more beyond!" Ever since it has been *plus ultra*.

> There's a land that is fairer than day,
>   And by faith we can see it afar;
> For the Father waits over the way,
>   To prepare us a dwelling place there.

Heaven! Oh, the grace of God that makes it possible!

I think of the Christian lady, on her deathbed, who asked someone to get a Bible and to read to her about Heaven. She said, "It is in the 14th chapter of John. Read it to me." So a loved one turned to the 14th chapter of John and started reading:

"Let not your heart be troubled"; he stopped and asked, "Is that it?"

She responded, "No, read on."

"Ye believe in God, believe also in me"; he stopped and inquired, "Is that it?"

"No, read on."

"In my Father's house are many mansions: if it were not so, I would have told you"; he stopped and asked again, "Is that it?"

No, read on."

"I go to prepare a place for you. And if I go and prepare a place for you, I will come again, and receive you unto myself"; he stopped and asked, "Is that it?"

She said, "No, read on."

"*...that where I am, there ye may be also.*"

She excitedly interrupted him, "Stop, that's it!" And he closed the Book.

Yes, that is *what* Heaven is: "*where I am, there ye may be also.*"

As Charles J. Butler, in his beautiful, "Where Jesus Is, 'Tis Heaven," expressed it:

> Once Heaven seemed a far-off place,
> Till Jesus showed His smiling face;
> Now it's begun within my soul,
> 'Twill last while endless ages roll.

Are you ready for Heaven? Are you *sure?* As that 14th chapter of John went on to quote our Lord Jesus Christ: "I am the way, the truth, and the life: no man cometh unto the Father, but by me" (Vs. 6). *That's it!* The way to Heaven is only through Christ and John 1:12 guarantees, "As many as received him, to them gave he power to become the sons of God, even to them that believe on his name." If you receive Him, Heaven *will* be yours!

In Sherman, Texas a teacher in the Beginner Department at the First Baptist Church asked the class what memorable event happened to them during the past week. Five-year-old Gary Jacobs answered immediately and positively. He announced, "My Daddy let me pour my own ketchup!"

No doubt that was a big event to him. Before you laugh too loudly, however, let me offer an opinion that the average adult, just as the little child, seems to have lost a sense of proper values. Mature men and women, who should know better, spend their time emphasizing the temporal and the material, while ignoring the spiritual and the eternal.

Jesus said, "For whosoever will save his life shall lose it: and whosoever will lose his life for my sake shall find it. For what is a man profited, if he shall gain the whole world, and lose his own soul? or what shall a man give in exchange for his soul?" (Matthew 16:24, 25).

Remember, there are more important things than pouring your own ketchup, and making sure your soul is saved for eternity is one of them. In fact, it is the *most important priority* you will ever have. Trust Him today. And if you do, we'd love to hear from you about it.

Conclusion

I was conducting services in a Michigan city that is home to one of the world's largest universities. On the Saturday night before the crusade closed, a 17-year-old high school senior, brought by friends, sat in the back of the center section. She did not respond to the invitation nor did she accept the pastor's offer of counseling when she left.

The next night, which closed the meeting, she had a movie date with a friend. When they returned to her home, her ex-sweetheart, a Korean veteran, the holder of a Silver Star for heroic action in the Pork Chop Hill fighting, was lying on his stomach on the other side of a neighbor's picket fence, cradling a rifle in his arms. When the couple approached the front door, the crazed suitor fired, hoping to hit the girl. Instead the bullet tore through the friend's heart, killing him instantly. He fired again and this time the slug severed one of the girl's main arteries.

She was rushed to the hospital where she underwent surgery and received numerous blood transfusions. After about three hours in the operating room she was pronounced "out of danger." Little did that girl know that within 24 hours after saying "No!" to Christ in an evangelistic crusade her date would be dead and she would be fighting for her life.

Because of this, it is very important to be ready when that sudden appointment with death arrives. Job reminds us about man, that "his days are determined, the number of his months are with thee, thou has appointed his bounds, that he cannot pass" (Job 14:5). Only the child of God can truly live without fear with reference to the approach of the Grim Reaper.

A sailor in the British Navy by the name of Sam Medley lived a wild and rebellious life without thought for God or his soul, seemingly. He was seriously wounded in a battle with the French and went to the home of his godly grandfather to recuperate. Since he had time on his hands with nothing much to do, he began to read the Word of God. It opened his eyes to the truth of his sin and its horrible hideousness. It also revealed the love of God as manifested in the death, burial and resurrection of Christ – and the free offer of His grace.

He soon made the great surrender and began to grow in the grace and knowledge of God's Son. Eventually he surrendered to the ministry and lived a useful life, working especially with sailors, for whom he had a great burden. When his time of departure arrived he said to those around his bedside, "I am a poor, shattered bark, just about to gain a blissful harbor. And, oh, how sweet will be the port after the storm! Dying is sweet, sweet work. My heavenly Father, I am looking up to my Christ, Jesus, my God, my Portion, my All in all."

Samuel Medley, who was born in 1738 and died in 1799, gave us this blessed song we still love to sing today, the tune we sing possibly adapted from one of Mozart's works:

> O could I speak the matchless worth,
> O could I sound the glories forth
> Which in my Savior shine,
> I'd soar and touch the heav'nly strings,
> And vie with Gabriel while he sings
> In notes almost divine,
> In notes almost divine.
>
> I'd sing the precious blood He spilt,
> My ransom from the dreadful guilt
> Of sin and wrath divine!
> I'd sing His glorious righteousness,
> In which all perfect heav'nly dress
> My soul shall ever shine,
> My soul shall ever shine.
>
> Well, the delightful day will come
> When my dear Lord will bring me home
> And I shall see His face;
> Then with my Savior, Brother, Friend,
> A blest eternity I'll spend,
> Triumphant in His grace,
> Triumphant in His grace.

Is that hope of Medley's your hope? Can you say you are confident your Savior, Brother, Friend, the Lord Jesus Christ, will receive you at death into His mansions of light? If not, the time to settle it is *right now!*

Postscript

The gates of Nehemiah 3 ended with the Gate Miphkad, which we saw was the Judgment Seat of Christ. Fortunately, that does not end the Christian life – *which will go on for eternity, as we saw in Chapter 12!*

Life for the unsaved will also go on for eternity. Alas, for them it will mean "unto the ages of the ages" in the Lake of Fire. Revelation 20:14, 15 put it like this: "And death and hell were cast into the lake of fire. This is the second death. And whosoever was not found written in the book of life was cast into the lake of fire."

God has done all! He can to keep the lost out of Hell and still maintain His holiness. They want their sin and so God simply grants them their desire, saying, "He that is unjust, *let him be unjust still*: and he which is filthy, *let him be filthy still* ..." (Revelation 22:11, emphasis added). They have no one to blame for their lost eternity but themselves.

However, I did not want to close this book without an appeal to any individual who has not been born again, or who questions whether or not he has had such a life-revolutionizing experience.

Let me be very, very clear: *anyone* can go to Heaven who *wants* to go to Heaven.

The Provision has Already Been Made!

It was *foretold* in Isaiah 53:5, 6: "He was wounded for our transgressions, he was bruised for our iniquities: the chastisement of our peace was upon him; and with his stripes we are healed ... and the LORD hath laid on him the iniquity of us all." Centuries before He was born of a Virgin, coming into this wicked and sinful world, it was prophesied exactly what He would do in taking our sins upon Himself, making a provision for us to be saved and saved forever.

The *fulfillment* came at Calvary when the Son of God died for the sins of all mankind. Romans 5:6-8 describes it: "For when we were yet without strength, in due time Christ died for the ungodly. For scarcely for a righteous man will one die: yet peradventure for a good man some would even dare to die. But God commendeth his love toward us, in that, while we were yet sinners, Christ died for us."

The horrors of the cross tell of God's great love for you and of the sacrifice His dear Son made to provide a "so great salvation" on your behalf. There is nothing more to do. Everything that *can* be done *has* been done! He did it *all*. As Christ said when He died, "It is finished" (John 19:30).

The Need is Obvious!

All of us are sinners – *wicked* sinners in His sight – since He is such a holy, sinless, perfect God. In that same Old Testament passage mentioned above we are told, "All we like sheep have gone astray; we have turned every one to his own way ..." (Isaiah 53:6). All of us have gone the way we wanted to go, ignoring His commands and wishes. And Ecclesiastes 7:20 adds, "There is not a just man upon earth, that doeth good, and sinneth not." His Word teaches there are no exceptions to this indictment of men, women, boys and girls.

The New Testament is just as strong in emphasizing our need. In Romans 3, after a blistering 14-fold indictment of our wickedness, the Apostle Paul summed it up: "... for there is no difference: For all have sinned, and come short of the glory of God." *No difference!* Indeed, we all have sinned and fallen short of His standard! Unless we have a Savior there is no hope for any of us.

While we are all sinners, not all are the same kind of sinners. Probably no one reading this far in this book would be like the farmer in Van Buren County (IL) years ago. The *Fort Madison Weekly Plaindealer* had a section "100 Years Ago" and on the date of June 9, 1860 a century previously it had reported the case of a man talking to his neighbor about the dry weather. Suddenly he began an outburst of the most terrible blasphemy, using the vilest epithets toward the Almighty and the Savior, because it did not rain.

The newspaper reported: ***"The man was going on in frightful lan-***
guage, when at once his jaws became palsied; his tongue became
powerless; his voice ceased; and he fell to the earth, a corpse."

God's judgment doesn't usually come that quickly or that sudden-ly, but come it does. You may not be guilty of such vile and venomous blasphemy, but remember the passage above declaring that we are *all* sinners – and that there is *no difference* in that fact! You need a Savior as surely as did he, or the most rabid blasphemer.

We cannot save ourselves. Ephesians 2:8, 9 expresses it: "For by grace are ye saved through faith; and that not of yourselves: it is the gift of God: Not of works, lest any man should boast." And Titus 3:3-6 adds, "But after that the kindness and love of God our Saviour toward man appeared, Not by works of righteousness which we have done, but according to his mercy he saved us, by the washing of regeneration, and renewing of the Holy Ghost; Which he shed on us abundantly through Jesus Christ our Saviour."

How clear is the Word of God that we cannot be saved by our own works, our own good deeds of righteousness – no matter how noble or how many.

What to Do

The action it takes to be saved is something any one can accomplish. The Bible describes it: "repentance toward God, and faith toward our Lord Jesus Christ" (Acts 20:21).

Repentance is an about face, a turnaround in the heart and mind. It indicates that the sinner, instead of going away from God toward Hell, turns toward God and starts toward Heaven. The word itself means "a change of mind." While that is primarily an inward decision, it is a little more than that, since it is a change of *mind* that involves a change of *action*.

This repentance involves and includes "faith toward our Lord Jesus Christ." This action of faith is highlighted repeatedly in the Word of God. Here are some examples:

The beloved John 3:16 and its context, "As Moses lifted up the serpent in the wilderness, even so must the Son of man be lifted up: That whosoever believeth in him should not perish, but have eternal life. For God so loved the world, that he gave his only begotten Son, that whosoever believeth in him should not perish, but have everlasting life. For God sent not his Son into the world to condemn the world; but that the world through him might be saved. He that believeth on him is not condemned: but he that believeth not is condemned already, because he hath not believed in the name of the only begotten Son of God" (Vss. 14-18).

"Be it known unto you therefore, men and brethren, that through this man is preached unto you the forgiveness of sins: And by him all that believe are justified from all things, from which ye could not be justified by the law of Moses" (Acts 13:38, 39).

And here is the promise on which I came to Christ and received personal salvation: "He came unto his own, and his own received him not. But as many as received him, to them gave he power to become the sons of God, even to them that believe on his name: Which were born, not of blood, nor of the will of the flesh, nor of the will of man, but of God" (John 1:11-13).

It is this simple. The very moment you receive Jesus Christ as Lord and Savior, you are guaranteed a Home in Heaven for eternity. As Romans 10:9-13 expresses it: "That if thou shalt confess with thy mouth the Lord Jesus, and shalt believe in thine heart that God hath raised him from the dead, thou shalt be saved. For with the heart man believeth unto righteousness; and with the mouth confession is made unto salvation. For the scripture saith, Whosoever believeth on him shall not be ashamed. For there is no difference between the Jew and the Greek: for the same Lord over all is rich unto all that call upon him. For whosoever shall call upon the name of the Lord shall be saved."

Will you call right now and be saved?

If you will, you can be assured of a Home in Heaven for all eternity. The Apostle Paul put it like this to those who believed at Thessalonica: "For God hath not appointed us to wrath, but to obtain salvation by our Lord Jesus Christ, Who died for us, that, whether we wake or sleep, we should live together with him" (I Thessalonians 5:9, 10). With Christ as Lord and Savior, it makes no difference whether you die or live. *You are His!*

If you do call on Him to save you, I would love to hear from you about your decision. I will send you a letter of counsel and encouragement about the Christian life. You may write me:

Dr. Robert L. Sumner
5717 Pine Drive
Raleigh, NC 27606

Testimonials

Dr. Robert Sumner's name is synonymous with integrity and excellence. This volume from God's faithful servant Nehemiah's book was conceived in the heart of the author and has been gestating for many years. Now, to our good and God's glory, it has been birthed for us to adopt these treasures and truths as our own. As the sweet Psalmist of Israel announced, we too can exclaim, "Lift up your heads O ye gates ... [that] the King of Glory may come in." As you journey through the "gates" of this volume a blessing awaits you. Read it and reap!

– Dr. O. S. Hawkins

You will not be far into the first few pages of this latest book from the pen of Robert L. Sumner before you feel like hollerin', "Preach it, brother!"

Here is all the passion of an evangelist combined with scholarly Bible teaching. Any reader who doesn't feel his heart stirred, his mind challenged, and his soul blessed as he pores over these pages needs to examine afresh the spiritual condition of his heart.

Readable, well-illustrated and Scriptural, this volume will provide any preacher with ideas for a score of sermons. And any lay-person who delves into this book will wish that he sat under this kind of ministry every Lord's Day.

Preach it, Brother! You surely can!

– Pastor Donald Prout

Bob Sumner has done it again. This prolific writer has penned another succinct, direct, Biblical, and useful volume for followers of Jesus Christ. All of us who are headed for that eternal gate to Heaven will be enabled and strengthened as we pass through our daily gates by reading this book.

– Dr. Paul Dixon

Here is a book of 187 pages, loaded with doctrinal illustrations!

He gives the reason, often overlooked, 500 were converted by Jonathan Edwards' great sermon, "Sinners in the Hands of an Angry God." That section on fasting and prayer moved my heart. Calling

God's people for concern for the terrible lapses of our day, and bringing to our attention Nehemiah's weeping, fasting and prayer as he was
called of God for the tremendous job in front of him.

With his heart on holy fire as though sweeping through a forest,
Dr. Sumner brings you through the book of Nehemiah – that kindled
first a flame in my heart that burned stronger as I read each page.
Starting at the Sheep Gate he takes us through the 10 gates mentioned
in Nehemiah 3 – showing how each one brings one to a deeper walk
with God.

The book is filled with thrilling illustrations – one that greatly
blessed my heart is the beautiful story behind the gospel song,
"Calvary Covers It All."

Sumner deals with a subject more and more omitted from pulpits
today – the reality of an everlasting Hell. His chapter on the "Old
Gate" needs to be read, and when you do, I believe you will want to
preach it. These sermons are from a heart on fire, as preached from
that heart, with an amazing number of illustrations, quotes, poems –
all together, bound to warm the reader's heart and bring him closer to
the Lord.

Sumner is a greatly devoted man of God who has served the Lord
faithfully and successfully over scores of years, blessed hearts and
encouraged ministers to faithfully serve God as he has done. He has
read widely and is a scholar of the highest level. This book will bless
and encourage your soul. It will be a blessing to you and would make
a wonderful gift to a pastor or a young person.

Though an inspirational book with many illustrations, it is a book
of sound Biblical doctrine. It deals in detail with the rapture, judgment seat of Christ, the marriage of the Lamb, and of the truth greatly
ignored – that of the believers' rewards. His last chapter, describing
Heaven, is the finest I have ever read on that subject, and of course,
as you would expect, he ends the book with a clear call for the decision to be made to call upon the Lord and live forever in that glorious
place prepared for the believer.

I recommend this book most highly. It is the type of message needed
today to fire our souls and give the growth in Christ.

– Dr. F. K. Beshore